A Brief History of Diaries:
From Pepys to Blogs

A Brief History of Diaries:

From Pepys to Blogs

Alexandra Johnson

Brief History
Published by Hesperus Press Limited
19 Bulstrode Street, London WIU 2JN
www.hesperuspress.com

First published by Hesperus Press Limited, 2011

Designed and typeset by Fraser Muggeridge studio
Printed and bound by CPI Group (UK) Ltd, Croydon CR0 4YY

ISBN: 978-1-84391-970-4

Contents

Introduction   9

First – Eighteenth Century: The Innovators   17
Ninth – Twentieth Century: Travel and Explorer Diaries   35
Eighteenth – Twentieth Century: Writers, Artists,
    Creative Diaries   55
Nineteenth – Twentieth Century: War Diaries   73
Twentieth – Twenty-First Century: Cyberspace
    and the Digital Diary   89

Bilbliography   103
Biographical note   107
Acknowledgements   109

To A.M.

Introduction

I never travel without my diary. One should always have some-thing sensational to read in the train.

– Oscar Wilde

At this moment three hardbound journals are still missing. One is sidetracked, possibly stranded in Mongolia, another buried deep in a private cupboard. The final one sits where it was left – on a train seat, still waiting for someone to pick it up. They are among the three that haven't yet found their way back to the 1000 Journals Project – one thousand blank journals left in random places all across the globe.

In August 2000, a graphic designer long fascinated by 'raw and spontaneous scribblings' started distributing blank journals in San Francisco – leaving them in cafes or on buses and benches. Each journal had instructions, inviting participants 'to contribute something and then pass it along to someone else'. They did. Diarists in forty countries soon were writing in a time-space continuum using three networks: 'face-to-face exchanges', the 'postal system – which is cheap and truly global', and the web 'to track and enliven the digital ghosts of the traveling books'.

Some entries recorded moments when the journals were passed on to another diarist – running with bulls in Pamplona; sailing down rivers on three continents. Others recorded a journal's strange fate – rescued in a law office or stolen at gunpoint.

'I left the journal on top of a Croatian mountain (Tuhobic) on July 30th. I hope that someone who cares will find it.' A year later the diarist in Journal 323 noted, 'The journal was still there. Mountaineers were using it as a sign-in book. So I took it with me and now it is somewhere in Zagreb.'

Most returned – the sheer inventive collaboration inside kept diarists from pocketing the journals, each handcrafted with an original cover design. A kind of living museum – diaries as found objects – the journals caught consciousness in motion. Diarists wrote, sketched, hand-stitched, pasted photos, drew captions, spray-painted stencils, inserted maps, rearranging continents. Using ink or watercolours, tiny print or solid block letters, they shared lives and stories – expressing, confessing, competing, connecting. In the serendipity of a moment who can resist shaping collective consciousness? The project and its three creative networks, after all, mirror the ever-evolving history of diaries as they continue launching themselves into the twenty-first century.

For a millennium diaries have fascinated the human imagination. In one of those three missing journals, someone could be scribbling any of these thoughts or facts:

iPhone's iDiary app stores multiple daily entries, all with encryption keys.

For centuries in the western region of China's Hunan province, women have written in Nushu, a secret language known only to them.

Scientists have calculated that 65,000 thoughts float through the mind daily.

In Japan those too busy to keep diaries can call in entries. The company sends a bound transcript at the end of the month.

The first online diary was Claudio Pinhanez's 'Open Diary', kept from 14 November 1994 until 1996.

'He who writes for himself writes to an eternal public.' – Ralph Waldo Emerson.

The longest diary is Robert Shields', an American minister, who entered the Guinness Book of Records in 2007 by writing 37.5 million words in diaries that fill ninety-one boxes. Recorded in five-minute segments, his diary is thirty times longer than Pepys'. (His father was the 1904 World Champion in speed typing.)

'It's like an oil change for the brain. A mental and biochemical tune-up.' – Dr Neil Neimark on the neuroscience of journal writing.

Samuel Johnson resolved fourteen times 'to keep a journal'. The first in 1760; the last in 1782.

'A journal is the ideal place of refuge for the inner self because it constitutes a counterworld: a world to balance the other.' – Joyce Carol Oates.

Journal is now a verb.

'I got out this diary and read, as one always reads one's own writing, with a kind of guilty intensity.' – Virginia Woolf.

The 1000 Journals Project bet on an irresistible truth: diaries are often more fun to read than to keep. 'It's not as easy as it looks,' warned the diarist in Journal 913. 'I've seen some AMAZING things in the pages of these journals. Just wait until it's your turn; and it keeps staring at you, calling to you.' Ten million journals are sold annually between October and December. Like New Year's resolutions, many will be abandoned by mid-January. Some only half-filled or blank after the opening page. It's as if that primal itch to record requires some special genetic wiring to complete its circuit. Yet for some diarists, even being unable to record is successfully noted. 'I do not remember this day,' Dorothy Wordsworth records for 17 March 1798. 'Such a beautiful day, that one felt quite confused how to make the most of it, and accordingly frittered it away,' Caroline Fox immortalised, 4 January 1848.

'I *love* to be *employed*; I hate to be *idle*,' Queen Victoria noted in her diary. For sixty-eight years she wrote almost daily in hers, the diary running to over one hundred volumes. Others have been less fortunate. For nineteen centuries, diaries have recorded, but they have also served as a constant reminder of intention and idleness. A nag, a rebuke, a private shame. The inability to keep them often provokes questioning of the genre itself. If, as Wilde suggests, 'memory is the diary that we all carry about with us', then trying to honour both memory and diary keeping often creates a love-hate relation unique to diarists.

Diaries. No genre is more misunderstood, more open to confusion and misinformation. That strange hybrid of recording and reflecting, confession and self-expression, no genre is more forced to justify itself. Mirror or window? Everyman's literature or narcissist's therapeutic habit? The question never deterred da Vinci, Darwin or Tolstoy. Or for that matter Kafka, Livingstone, Thoreau, Delacroix, Byron, Camus, Sassoon, Boswell, Plath, Gauguin, Dostoevsky, Woolf, Warhol. The list is endless. They were too busy using diaries, journals and notebooks for their own work to quibble about diary keeping. Pepys may be its most famous practitioner, but that honour is now being challenged daily by millions of digital diarists and bloggers. In our twenty-first-century linked, tell-all culture, keyboards click away, undermining Siegfried Sassoon's observation that, 'When all is said and done, leading a good life is better than keeping a good diary.'

Over a millennium, diaries have survived and thrived – from the mulberry branch used by the Chinese to produce paper well into a paperless world in the digital era. No small feat. A diary has no user's manual but *hundreds* of unwritten rules. Those hissing shoulds: keep a diary daily; write only in hardbound journals; record only deep thoughts in perfect handwriting. None of it was a problem in *Journal d'un Bourgeois de Paris*, kept between 1409 and 1431. Or for the eleventh-century Irish monk who wrote despite 'the cold' on his hands. Both wrote anonymously. So for centuries have most diarists. Who are they? As Thomas Mallon notes, 'Some are chroniclers of the everyday. Others have kept their books only in special times – over the course of a trip, or during a crisis. Some have used them to record journeys of the soul, plan the art of the future, confess the sins of the flesh, lecture the world from beyond the grave. And some of them, prisoners and invalids, have used them not so much to record lives as create them.'

For centuries both the famous and the anonymous have discovered the creative and psychic pull of diaries. Kafka: 'Writing is the axe that breaks the frozen sea within.' Joan Didion: 'Some morning when the world seems drained of wonder, some day when I am only going through the motions of doing what I'm supposed to do, which I write – on that bankrupt morning I will simply open my notebook and there it will be, a forgotten account with accumulated interest paid back to the world out there.'

'What is a diary as a rule?' wondered Ellen Terry. 'A document useful to the person who keeps it, dull to the contemporary who reads it, invaluable to the student, centuries afterwards, who treasures it!' Let's clarify a few misconceptions about diary keeping that have plagued diarists past and present. Diary or journal? Both words come from the Latin root for 'day'. But ever since Samuel Johnson defined diary in his *Dictionary* as 'an account of the transactions, accidents and observation of every day; a journal', they've been used interchangeably. For purists, a diary is a daily factual record, dated and chronological. A journal is kept more fitfully and for deeper reflection. One records, the other reflects. Twitter now does both.

Whether keeping a hardbound journal or a digital Open Diary, every diarist still aspires to the one Virginia Woolf imagined. 'What sort of diary would I like mine to be? Something loose knit... so elastic that it will embrace anything, solemn, slight or beautiful that comes into my mind. I should like it to resemble some deep old desk, or capacious hold-all, in which one flings a mass of odds & ends... I should like to come back, after a year or two, and find that the collection had sorted itself.'

The reasons for keeping diaries are as varied as human nature itself. Is it just for oneself? Or always with an eye for posterity? Francis Kilvert, the English country curate, did both when writing in 1870–9: 'Why do I keep this voluminous journal? I can hardly tell. Partly because life appears to me such a curious and wonderful thing that it seems a pity that even such a humble and uneventful life as mine should pass altogether away without some such record… and partly too because I think the record may amuse and interest some who come after me.' The mild parson vividly described rural life, resisting the temptations of egotism and self-censorship. Of his twenty-two notebooks, only three survived, the rest destroyed first by his wife and then by the niece who inherited them. Now considered a classic, Kilvert's surviving diary was published in three volumes.

Secrecy. Over the centuries, diarists have found ingenious ways to hide and protect journals so they can write freely. Da Vinci wrote in mirror-reverse handwriting. Pepys kept his in cipher. Beatrix Potter kept hers in code. John Dee, the Elizabethan mathematician, used Greek and Latin for his first and second wives. Anaïs Nin kept two sets of diaries, one for each husband. Japanese pillow books are still slipped under heads and away from prying eyes.

Even the digital diarist often first started with a hardbound lock-and-key diary. Memoirist Patricia Hampl's first diary was one of those 'red leatherette five-year diaries, bolted shut by a diminutive brass lock whose ineffectual key I hid elaborately in my bedroom. A journal not only required secrecy – it was secrecy. My brother, idly curious, didn't even bother to search for the little key; he coolly sprang the lock with a bent paper clip, and laughed himself silly. My first reader.'

'Whom do I tell when I tell a blank page?' wondered Virginia Woolf. Oneself, of course. 'True to oneself – which self?' Katherine Mansfield mused. Diaries expose the human instinct to magnify or diminish the psyche. 'This journal is a relief,' Byron observed. 'When I am tired – as I generally am – out comes this and down goes everything. But I can't read it over: and God knows what contradictions it may contain. If I am sincere with myself (but I fear one lies more to one's self than to anyone else)...'

Certainly some of the world's most famous diaries are notoriously unreflective. As Parisians stormed the Bastille, Louis XVI's diary records only a single word of what was noteworthy that day: 'Rien!' (Nothing!) In the final months before the Russian Revolution, Tsar Nicholas II noted cloud formations, subtle drops in weather pressure. Power doesn't always give rise to subtle introspection. Queen Victoria kept diaries. So did Che Guevara. Queen Victoria's daughter Beatrice transcribed her mother's 1837–1901 notebooks, editing and deleting passages, then destroying the originals.

They probably weren't state secrets that Beatrice censored but what Virginia Woolf called 'the dumps and the dismals'. In the heat of the moment, a diarist drops the public mask and writes with rare candour. 'I seem to write in it only when I am depressed,' Barbara Pym noted, 'like praying only when one is really in despair.' Yet Elizabeth Freake intentionally used her diary as strategic grudge. Its cover reads, 'Mrs Elizabeth Freake her diary 1671 to 1714 some few remembrances of my misfortuns which have attended me in my unhappy life since I were marryd wch was November 14, 1671.' She signed each entry like an affidavit.

Occasionally, some unreflective diaries are noteworthy for missing what another diarist would record as important. In 1793 Irish schoolmaster John Fitzgerald records criminals being executed. 'They arrived at the gallows at 5:10 p.m., and were cut down at 6:30. It was a charming evening, dry and the sun shining, though there were several showers in the morning. Johnny and I went to the Shinnicks and saw the execution.'

Too often diarists over the centuries have unwisely measured theirs against da Vinci's 5,000-page notebooks. His boundless curiosity filled page after page with ideas and plans for inventions and philosophical observations: 'This is to be a collection without order, taken from many papers, which I have copied here, hoping afterwards to arrange them according to the subjects.' Over forty years he'd discovered what the earliest private diaries soon practised – giving a diary a single purpose, something put into practice in the earliest religious, travel and military diaries.

Like Leonardo's notebooks, diaries soon served as cunning little archives or storehouses for explorers, scientists, artists and writers. Darwin's fifteen notebooks contained the research that revolutionised science; Woolf used her diaries to plan nine novels; Delacroix's journals were kept as both sketchpads and ongoing reflections on his painting.

The majority of diaries, though, capture the life of Everyman. 'A journal keeper is really the natural historian of his own life,' observes Verlyn Klinkenborg. 'But many of the great journals are marked by a dogged absence of self-consciousness, a willingness to suspend judgment of the journal itself.' From their earliest start as records of conscience straight through to today's culture of confession, diarists have mapped the history of self-awareness itself.

No matter what their form or type, diaries are the living embodiment of E.M. Forster's famous dare: only connect. For over a millennium, diaries have allowed individuals to connect first within themselves and then with the larger world. 'Someday journals will have chips in them, making their location clearer,' notes the 1000 Journal Project. Until then, diaries continue to map consciousness, offering the world a rich, complex and truthful account of what it means to be human.

First – Eighteenth Century:
The Innovators

Diarists, that shrewdly innocent breed, those secret exhibitionists and incomparable purveyors of the sequential, self-conscious life.
— Gail Godwin

In AD 105, Ts'ai Lun, chief eunuch in Ho Ti's court, unveiled a new invention: paper. Like gunpowder and moveable type which the Chinese later gave civilisation, paper was a truly revolutionary gift. Initially, the imperial court was sceptical of this strange mix of animal and plant fibres. For centuries, people had been content to keep daily records on silk and bamboo slips. Impatient, Ts'ai Lun feigned his own death, having himself secretly buried alive in a coffin. A hollow bamboo pole allowed him to breathe. Mourners were told to grieve by burning imitation money. Suddenly, a piece of paper shot up through the hollow bamboo pole. A sign. The gods favoured this new invention. As Ts'ai Lun opened the coffin, he provided the world with a fitting image for the diarist: someone hidden, shooting paper into the dark, hoping others are noticing as he emerges.

The instinct to record daily life and thoughts is as ancient as handwriting. Some forms of diaries survive chiselled in cuneiform. Hand painted in hieroglyphs. Etched on wooden tablets. The history of diaries is the history of consciousness itself. Its dates are inevitably tied to inventions such as paper and print, and now microchip, which have allowed daily private records to survive in vast numbers. If innumerable ancient diaries have been lost, it's not surprising that those that survived were kept by diarists most able to ensure their protection and longevity. The earliest diarists had something significant to record – history itself.

Marcus Aurelius' twelve-book *Meditations*, 'thoughts/writings addressed to himself', is often credited as the first surviving diary. Written in Greek between AD 170 and 180 while he was on military campaign, it consists mostly of one- or two-sentence epigrams or reflections. It establishes the motivation of every diary to follow: to record, to reflect, and, above all, to improve the self. Its maxims underscore a diary's promise of transformation and self-reinvention. Aurelius, the Stoic, takes aim at the future spoilers of the form. Brooders. Complainers. 'A cucumber is bitter. Throw it away. There are briars in the road. Turn aside from them... And do not add, "Why were such things made in the world."' For Aurelius, recording the inner life is given a deeper impetus: the diary as hourglass: 'Do not act as if you were going to live a thousand years,' one of the *Meditations* cautions, 'soon you'll be ashes or bones. A mere name at most – and even that is just a sound – an echo.'

That echo – leaving a name and proof of having lived – has impelled diarists ever since. Some of the earliest notational diaries come from the Arab world. In Europe, thanks to Silk Route trade, diaries first surfaced in cultures with the earliest papermaking centres. Diary keeping took deepest root in Italy, where paper production exploded, most notably in the two cities with early printing presses: Florence and Venice.

Modern diary keeping owes its origins to the fifteenth-century culture of accounting. Since the thirteenth century, some form of *ricordanze*, diary-like accounting books, had inventoried every aspect of public and private life. From the military to matrimony to monasteries, northern Italian cities were awash with *ricordanze*. Inevitably, an accounting culture of debts and assets inspired the logical shift from finance to conscience. Diaries were a new form of a balance sheet. In Medieval and

Renaissance Europe, the earliest diarists came from the literate ruling or political elite. Privilege had put them in the advantageous position of eyewitnesses. Diarists were both observers of and participants in the opening of international trade routes and the expansion of financial markets. Merchant bankers often kept diaries, such as that of Buonaccorso Pitti between 1354 and 1432, whose entries mix thoughts on warfare in France with notes on gambling losses or profits from saffron, wine and horse-trading.

Inevitably, diaries began the slow shift from recording public life to mediating on private concerns. Pitti's fellow patrician politician, Lapo Niccolini (1356–1463), is one of the first chroniclers to drop the public mask. He fastidiously records losing family members to plague; a first wife to childbirth; the fate of his son, Otto, born without a left hand. Niccolini's factual entries – calculating shop rental incomes and properties – are soon balanced by moral reflections. On 13 December 1417, clear-eyed as an accountant, Niccolini takes inventory after the death of his son Niccolaio: 'He had neither wife nor children, and he made no will,' the diarist records. 'He had dissipated and wasted more of my substance than was lawfully his... he was too great a spendthrift of his own and others' money. He cared for nothing but the gratification of his desires... and he gave me a great deal of trouble while he lived in this miserable world.' Niccolini records a son's failure while asserting his own virtuous life.

Niccolini's other children inherited diary keeping as a family legacy. From 1429 on, there is a wealth of recorders within the family. His sixth son, Paolo, was a dedicated recorder of private life in Renaissance Italy. Inspired perhaps by his own three marriages, he has left one of the most extensive portraits of Renaissance weddings in any private diary. For the 1459 wedding of his daughter Ginevra, he catalogues her sixty-item trousseau, including sets of intricately embroidered wedding sheets. Clothes detailed in his diary are immortalised in Ghirlandaio's frescoes of Ginevra in Santa Maria Novella. His diary records the wedding *torta*, a pie layered with pork, chicken, ham, mixed with onion, dates, almonds, sugar and saffron. Giustina Niccolini took the family tradition a step further: chronicling the history of an institution. When she entered Le Murate as a Benedictine nun in the 1570s, she stepped into the great recording culture of Florence's convents. Just as four generations of Niccolini diarists had recorded Florence's political and intellectual life, she became a private chronicler of Le Murate's role in providing the small writing rooms for scribes and recorders like herself.

The first modern diary – as we would most recognise it – was written neither by a patrician merchant banker or a convent scribe. Luca Landucci, a Florentine apothecary, kept a diary from 1450 to 1516. It was continued by an unknown hand, most likely his son, until 1542. Written in his apothecary shop on Canto de' Tornaquinci, it's the first surviving diary in which we hear the voice of the ordinary private citizen. Just as the human face was moving into the foreground of Renaissance paintings, so with Landucci a private voice full of nuance surfaces in a diary.

Landucci, an accountant's son, had a natural instinct for inventory keeping. Instead of noting his birthdays towards the start of his diary, he lists the number of popes (five) who have come and gone by the time he's twenty-two. Towards the end of the diary, he marks six decades by describing the permanent switch in men's fashions, from long to short hair, from hoods to hats. It's the rich social inventory of the city, though, that his diary catalogues: the first sugar from Madera; new silver coins minted for taxes; boys playing a game of *palla* on the frozen Arno; a hunt staged in the Piazza de' Signoria in 1514, the square teeming with imported wild lions, bears and leopards.

The diary is a magnifying glass of daily Renaissance life – held up not from the isolated and precarious seats of power, but by an ordinary citizen walking Florence's narrow streets. Landucci notes artists from Donatello to Andrea del Castagno. But it's the city's scientific preoccupation with anatomy that fascinates him. Landucci attends hangings with punctuality bordering on civic duty. The diarist's eye is shaped by scientific objectivity. He records medical professors petitioning for the corpse of a young man who'd just been hanged. As an apothecary, he's ideally situated to receive reliable first-hand information. Fact, not gossip, prevails. With the same cool scientific eye of the university doctors interested in dissection, Landucci writes of a hermit suspected of assassinating Lorenzo de' Medici. On 15 October 1481, Landucci notes: 'they skinned his feet, and then burnt them by holding them in the fire till the fat dripped off them; after which they set him upright and made him walk across the great hall; and these things caused his death. Opinions were divided as to whether he was guilty or innocent.'

Landucci's diary is a landmark in the early history of diaries for another reason. It was later passed from hand to hand, copied numerous times, taken to Siena and then throughout Tuscany. It's easy to see why. It presents the unfolding drama of a city and church perpetually under siege from reform. Landucci offers a satisfying mix of the powerful and the penitent, the spiralling reversal of fortunes for church and state alike. His diary chronicles the city's most historic events, among them the Pazzi conspiracy, the botched assassination of members of the Medici during high mass on 26 April 1478; the stoking of the Bonfire of the Vanities on 27 February 1497, to rid the city of its excess and distractions. One of its most gripping entries is the eye-witness account of Savonarola being burned at the stake. The Dominican monk and reformer stood accused of heresy for challenging both church and government. With cinematic clarity, Landucci describes as Savonarola and two other friars are led to the platform on 22 May 1498.

No single entry better captures Landucci's eye for scientific observation and the crowd's thirst for the miraculous. While all eyes are on the platform, his are on the crowd. It's less the hanging that horrifies the crowd than the friars' utter silence up until that moment. The crowd stays hushed 'as everyone had been expecting some signs'. It's the drama of the disappointed, some in the crowd losing their faith and others witnessing the death of a true martyr. Gunpowder placed under the circular platform is lit, 'the fire burst out with the noise of rockets and cracking', consuming the three friars.

> In a few hours they were burnt, their legs and arms gradually dropping off; part of their bodies remaining hanging to the chains, a quantity of stones were thrown to make them fall, as there was a fear of the people getting hold of them; and then the hangman and those whose business it was, hacked down the post and burnt it on the ground, bringing a lot of brushwood, and stirring the fire up over the dead bodies so that the very last piece was consumed. Then they fetched carts, and accompanied by mace-bearers, carried the last bit of dust to the Arno, by the Ponte Vecchio, in order that no remains should be found. Nevertheless, a few good men had so much faith that they gathered some of the floating ashes together, in fear and secrecy, because it was as much as one's life was worth to say a word, so anxious were the authorities to destroy every relic.

The earliest diaries, including da Vinci's notebooks, dutifully record natural catastrophes. Both Niccolini and Landucci note eclipses, flooding, freak lightning strikes. The entries often shade into the superstitious – seeing ill omens, for example, in Siamese twins or children born with birth defects. As diary keeping took hold in Europe, especially in England, recording natural disasters was safer than chronicling the political turmoil they symbolised. Nowhere is that more evident than in sixteenth- and seventeenth-century diaries kept during the turbulent Reformation years. Diaries were both the natural result of – and often the only private response to – the chaotic, cleansing effects of Catholic and Protestant reform movements. Diarists constantly recorded wars or imagined the end of the world.

Apocalyptic fears spawned that singular diarist, mathematician, scientist philosopher, John Dee, who kept diaries from 1577–1601. When Dee began his most famous surviving diary in 1577, he had just finished a treatise on the principles of navigation. In it, he coined the term 'British Empire', envisioning not just geographical but cultural expansion. England would be the New Jerusalem. Begun first as scientific and court notations, his diary reflects back on 1544, recording eminent Elizabethans, among them Raleigh, Sidney and Dudley. Dee records his service as an influential adviser offering technical and mathematical support for English voyages through the 1570s. His diary shows Dee as another kind of celestial navigator. Using a private symbol for Queen Elizabeth, he notes that she 'promised unto me great security, against any of her kingdom that would, by reason of any of my rare studies and philosophical exercises, unduly seek my overthrow'.

Dee mathematically navigated by stars and read destiny in them. He had found favour with Queen Elizabeth after calculating the auspicious day for her 1558 coronation. Thereafter he consulted the stars for signs for her – and England's – health. His diary notes the many, including Elizabeth, who travelled to Richmond to seek his counsel. Dee had written the influential preface to Euclid's *Elements* and had the largest private library in England. Some 600 people are recorded in his diary. Dee was probably the only diarist in history to leave both chemistry and spirit diaries. In 1582 he finds an ambitious intention for diary keeping: *Medicina Dei*, 'medicine of God', to cure an ailing civilisation. With the help of alchemist assistants, the deeply religious Dee kept a 'colloquium of angels' diary. Over nine years he recorded information the archangels offered, some forty-eight divine keys, to purify the Christian world. As late as 1583, Dee's spirit diaries were kept to alert sovereigns, including Emperor Rudolf II, of imminent threats.

An early entry offers good news from above for explorers, 'the corners and straights of the earth shall be measured to the depth: and strange shall be the wonders that are creeping in to new worlds.' But Elizabethan England was rife with spies and traitors. Dee hid diaries, buried others, kept one in a chimney. 'This book, and holy key, which unlocketh the secrets of God,' an entry cautions, 'is so holy that I wonder why it is delivered to those that shall decay.' Dee's diaries offer an important transitional link between religion and science. Like any diarist, he worries about the diaries' legacy. 'And in those 28 volumes there were 48 individual books, most mystical (as God himself is witness) of greater value than all things in the world are worth. For in them were contained an admirable wisdom and divine power which we, at God's good time, must use to his honour and glory.'

On 29 September 1600, Dee burned nine years' worth of diaries. One page survives of his 'Compendious Rehearsal', which records the noteworthy events over forty-five years, many made as single notations. Only the first volume of the spirit diaries survives. After his death in 1604, a London confectioner inherited a cedar chest. In a secret drawer he found the surviving spirit diary manuscript. An overzealous kitchen maid subsequently used pages from the diary manuscript to line pie plates.

'The history of diary-writing, in so far as it exists, is that of the development of self-awareness,' notes Phillip Spalding. 'It is the rise of nationality, and within nations the rise of individual consciousness, under the twin spurs of freedom of thought through the Renaissance of classical learning, and freedom of conscience in the Reformation, that prepare the way for autobiography of all kinds.' The alchemy of human spirit that eluded Dee is achieved by a fellow navigational expert and diarist. Nowhere is diary as autobiography more brilliantly first shown than in the pages of Samuel Pepys, the inventor of the truly modern diary. In Pepys' hands the diary becomes a kind of camera, experimenting with long and close-up lenses.

When the twenty-seven-year-old Pepys made his first entry in 1660, cheap pocket almanacs and the rise of print culture had already been instrumental in boosting diary keeping in England. Puritan diaries stressed conscience and confession – writing daily about the self as a way to *transcend* it. 'A narrow examination of thy selfe and the course of thy life,' as William Perkins advised. Yet in Quaker and other Dissenter diaries the focus soon included gratitude. Daily life was to be celebrated. The proliferation of diary keeping in the late seventeenth century coincided with the rise of literacy and the increase in foreign travel. The diarist's ability to record his epoch was now shaped by an expanded sense of how to see it.

With Pepys the diary shifted from Eye to I. Nothing is lost on Pepys. His eye for detail notes his wife's new 'pair of gloves trimmed with yellow ribbon' or their supper of mutton and marrow bones and an anchovy tart. The effect is tumult, detail after detail, that mimic Pepys' sheer appetite for life. Pepys is the ideal diarist – keenly observant yet unself-conscious. Pepys displays an endless childlike delight in exploring the immediate world with bounding curiosity. He shows no hesitation when recording his thrill at a new watch which he checks 'a hundred times' during a coach ride. He strips himself of vanity, including when most vain about new clothes. He willingly shows himself to be a clueless husband, 'waking this morning out of my sleep on a sudden, I did with my elbow hit my wife a great blow over her face and nose, which waked her with pain, at which I was sorry, and so to sleep again'. His candour is a virtue even if his acts are not. He refuses to hide his regret that kissing a homely woman is a loss of valuable time.

Pepys began his diary on 1 January 1660 in his Axe Yard house near Whitehall. He had been newly appointed Clerk of the Acts in the Naval Office that oversaw the royal dockyards. Later he became Chief Secretary to the Admiralty and a key naval administrator, yet his fame is his diary. Between 1660–9, missing only a fortnight in 1668, he wrote 3,102 pages – one and a half million words – all kept in secret shorthand. Pepys is the ideal companion and guide to tumultuous Restoration London. From

Charles II's court to his own kitchen, from his Navy office to the docks, he provides a portrait of seventeenth-century life, both as participant and spectator. The diary's immediacy is its constant present-tense activity – watching the king play tennis; angling a good spot to watch a hanging; singing in the coach with his wife; playing nine pins with Lord Admiral Montagu; noting the stench from his uncle's casket; blackening a cook's eye.

His diary is a tapestry of hundreds of scenes, including the most historic – the 1665 Plague and the Great Fire of 1666. In both, London itself is a character. Pepys' reportorial eye notes the plague's slow-building drama. On 7 June 1665 he sees 'two or three houses marked with a red cross upon the doors, and "Lord have mercy upon us" writ there'. He observes a ship-silent Thames, grass growing up and down Whitehall's deserted streets. By August, 'In the City died this week 7,496; and of them 6,102 of the plague. But it is feared that the true number of the dead this week is near 10,000 – partly from the poor that cannot be taken notice of through the greatness of their number.' Pepys stayed in London while doctors and politicians fled. By late August, he notes only 'one apothecary left – all being dead'.

His entries are sketched obituaries. On 14 September 1665 he rues seeing someone 'sick of the sores carried close by me by Grace-church in a hackney coach – my finding the Angell tavern at the lower end of Tower-hill shut up; and more then that, the alehouse at the Tower-stairs; and more then that, that the person was then dying of the plague when I was last there, a little while ago at night'. Pepys writes of seeing 'poor Dr Burnets door shut. But he hath, I hear, gained great goodwill among his neighbours, for he discovered it himself first, and caused himself to be shut up of his own accord – which was very handsome.' Walking at night, he notes, 'two women, crying and carrying a man's coffin between them'.

From his office windows he watches London's timber-framed houses ignite in the 1666 Great Fire.

Staid till it was dark almost and saw the fire grow; and as it grew darker appeared more and more; and in corners and upon steeples and between churches and houses as far as we could see up the hill of the City in a most horrid, malicious, bloody flame not like the fine flame of an ordinary fire... we saw the fire as only one entire arch of fire from this to the other side of the bridge and in a bow up the hill for an arch above a mile long; it made me weep to see it.

Another civil war – one erupting in Pepys' own crowded home – is carefully recorded. Pepys' diary is dominated by turbulent quarrels and reconciliations with his wife, Elizabeth. 'Lay long in bed talking with my wife,' begin many entries. Pepys confesses the 'strange slavery that I stand in to beauty'. His entry for 27 September 1667 changes his life and gives the diary its interior storyline. 'My wife sends for me to come to home, and what was it but to see the pretty girl which she is taking to wait upon her; and though she seems not altogether so great a beauty as she had before told me, yet indeed she is mighty pretty; and so pretty, that I find I shall be too much pleased with it, and therefore could be contented as to my judgment, though not to my passion, that she might not come, lest I may be found too much minding her, to the discontent of my wife.'

Seventeen-year-old Deborah Willet is at the centre of matrimonial warfare. November's entries record Pepys on his knees, his wife raging in the couple's blue bedroom, forcing him to dismiss her maid. On 20 November he must first 'write to [Deb] that I hated her'. Without his wife's knowledge, Pepys gives Deb money, coming after her in the street. By January, he notes, 'this evening I observed my wife mighty dull; and I myself was not mighty fond.' As late as 19 April 1669 Pepys wonders in his diary if he'd see or pass Deb in Westminster: 'I know not; but she not appearing.'

In his preface to the diaries, Robert Louis Stevenson notes that Pepys was also 'a serious-minded business man, and conscientious public servant, clever, shrewd and painstakingly, if not brilliant, and honest as men with his opportunities'. With his reporter's eye and the soul of a gossip, Pepys used his opportunities to move diary keeping from confession to self-expression and then into the realm of literature. Pepys' habit of making rough notes and later shaping and polishing them is evident as early as 10 November 1665. 'Enter all my Journal since the 28 of October, having every day's passage well in my head, though it troubles me to remember it; and what I was forced to, being kept from my lodging, where my books and papers are, for several days.' The sketched entries owe equally to the diarist's keen eye but also to memory and his shaping hand. As Pepys' biographer Claire Tomalin observes, 'He knows how to shape the material, where to linger, where to give a piece of direct speech, where to hurry on.'

A prolific reader, Pepys read late at night, his eyes strained by candlelight but also by the diary's cipher shorthand. Fearing that he was losing his sight, on 31 May 1669 Pepys made the diary's final entry:

And thus ends all that I doubt I shall ever be able to do with my own eyes in the keeping of my Journal, I being not able to do it any longer, having done now so long as to undo my eyes almost every time that I take a pen in my hand; and, therefore, whatever comes of it, I must forebear: and, therefore, resolve, from this time forward, to have it kept by my people in long-hand, and must therefore be contented to set down no more than is fit for them and all the world to know... I must endeavour to keep a margin in my book open, to add, here and there, a note in short-hand with my own hand.

And so I betake myself to that course, which is almost as much as to see myself go into the grave: for which, and all discomforts that will accompany my being blind, the good God prepare me!

On 26 May 1703, diarist John Evelyn wrote of 'his particular friend'. Learning of Pepys' death, he recalled 'a very worthy, Industrious & curious person'. From their correspondence Evelyn already knew Pepys' curious habits, notably his stonefest, the annual supper celebrating the removal of his kidney stones. As diarists, the two are often paired. Both were courtiers known to Charles II, both held important administrative posts during the Restoration – Evelyn the Commissioner for Prisoners of War during the Dutch conflicts. But they are opposites. Evelyn is consciously introspective to Pepys' spontaneous extrovert. Evelyn's diary spanned nearly three-quarters of a century – chronicling five reigns, the Civil Wars, the Restoration and the Revolution of 1688. Evelyn took to rewriting many of his 1640–1706 diary entries to serve as notes for a future memoir.

Evelyn's diary owes its habit of detailed entries to the spirit of John Beadle's *The Journal or Diary of a Thankful Christian* (1656). Such diaries were aids to spiritual self-discipline, recording instances of God's 'deliverances'. Puritan diarists were urged to examine not just their conscience, but a diary's entries for *patterns* of God's sustaining guidance. Evelyn's entries on the Great Fire assume apocalyptic meaning. On 2 September 1666 he records:

Oh miserable and calamitous spectacle! Such as haply the world had not seen since the foundation of it, nor be outdone till the universal conflagration thereof. All the sky was of a fiery aspect, like the top of a burning oven, and the light seen above 40 miles about for many nights. God grant mine eyes may never behold the like, who now saw above 10,000 houses all in one flame; the noise and cracking and thunder of people, the fall of towers, houses, and churches, was like an hideous storm, and the air all about so hot and inflamed that at last one was not able to approach it, so that they were forced to stand still and let the flames burn on, which they did for near two miles in length and one in breadth. The clouds also of smoke were dismal and reached upon computation near 50 miles in length. Thus I left it this afternoon burning, a resemblance of Sodom, or the last day. It forcibly called to my mind that passage – *non enim hic habemus stabilem civitatum*; the ruins resembling the picture of Troy. London was, but is no more! Thus, I returned.

On 3 September punishment is literally raining down on London. 'The stones of Paul's flew like grenados the melting lead running down the streets in a stream and the very pavements glowing with fiery redness so no horse or man was able to tread on them.' A week before the Great Fire Evelyn had offered suggestions as to how to reinforce St Paul's Cathedral. In Evelyn's diaries, his level of anxiety is measured by the frequent entries on inventions destined to save civilisation: silk-weaving engines, mechanical clocks, industrial paper mills. 'A lover of the sea and skillful in shipping,' he writes approvingly of Charles II, 'he had a laboratory and knew many empirical medicines and the easier mathematics; he loved planting and building.'

His diaries put in what official documents or letters must omit: secrets and politically incorrect opinions, such as his distaste for Charles II's dissipated court. The rise of late seventeenth-century diary keeping coincided with the growth of print culture. Yet seismic political and religious upheavals forced diarists like Evelyn – and later John Wesley and George Fox – to turn inward, reflecting on the ever-shifting world. Evelyn had witnessed the deaths of both Charles I and Cromwell. One of his diary's most singular entries records an ominously portentous sight.

This evening looking out my Chamber Window towards the West, I first saw a Meteor (or what ever Phaenomenon it was) of an obscure bright Colour (if so I may call it without a solecism) resembling the brightness of the Moone when under a thin Clow'd, very much like the blade of a sword... What this may Portend (for it was very extraordinaire) God onely knows; but such another Phaenomen I remember I saw, which went North to South, and was much brighter, and larger... proceeding our bloody Rebellion. I pray God avert his Judgments; we have had of late severall Comets, which though I believe appeare from natural Causes... They may be warnings from God, as they commonly are fore-runners of his Annimadversions.

In 1762 a shy, often melancholic comet of a diarist struck London. When twenty-two-year-old James Boswell began his *London Journal*, confession and cosmic judgement were altered forever. In Boswell's brilliant, hedonistic diaries, he is wrestling with two angels: ambition and his place in recording history. His 1760–95 journals provided the raw material for the books that won him fame: *Journal of a Tour to the Hebrides*, *Journal of a Tour to Corsica*, and *The Life of Samuel Johnson*, many of its scenes lifted directly from the journals. With Boswell, the diarist is equally – or more – important than what is being recorded. Like Pepys and Evelyn at the hub of political life, Boswell was a fixture in London's literary and social celebrity culture. Its star, Samuel Johnson, 'advised me to keep a journal of my life, fair and undis-guised'. For 8,000 pages, he did just that, an irresistible mix of travel, scandal and celebrity. Boswell is the first celebrity diarist, self-styled, writing with an eye to posterity, less to confess as impress.

Boswell's 1762–3 *London Journal* records his first meeting Johnson, as well as his own future mistress, Louisa. In its preface he writes, 'the ancient philosopher certainly gave a wise counsel when he said "Know thyself"... I have therefore determined to keep a daily journal in which I shall set down my various senti-ments and my various conduct... It will give me a habit of application and improve me in expression.' Until Boswell, con-fession and sober self-examination shadowed diaries. In John Wesley's eight-volume 1725–91 diaries, the evangelist founder of Methodism often wrote in the third person so he 'might see in black and white and to be in a position to judge accurately as to his own motives, attainments, doings and failures'. Boswell revolutionised diaries by parting the curtain, often writing in the intimate second person familiar – the *you* being both himself and the reader over his shoulder.

'As a lady adjusts her dress before a mirror, a man adjusts his character by looking at his journal,' Boswell mused. 'One great object which I have ever,' he wrote, 'has been to obtain the acquaintance, and if possible, the regard, of Rousseau.' Long before 2 December 1764 when he met the author of the *Confessions*, Boswell had liberated the first person singular in diaries. It was now the agent – rather than the subject – of confession. If Pepys is Everyman, then Boswell is Every Ambition. The subversive pleasure of his diaries is the sheer liveliness of his desires. In seventeenth-century confessional diaries, as Phillip Spalding notes, 'the venial errors are paraded, the real sins pass unnoticed or are suppressed'. Boswell parades his with a gusto that rivals Pepys' roving eye – seductions, philandering, hangovers.

The conversational brilliance of Johnson's London animates the journals. Boswell often writes entries as a witty one-act play, the actors' names boldfaced. In his *London Journal* he confronts his mistress for giving him gonorrhoea. 'Boswell: Pray, Madam, in what state of health have you been for some time?' With similar brio, he records his first encounter with the fifty-four-year-old compiler of the *Dictionary of the English Language*:

[Boswell] Mr Johnson, I do indeed come from Scotland, but I cannot help it.
[Johnson] That, sir, I find, is what a great many of your countrymen cannot help.

Boswell, notes Phillip Spalding, often writes of himself as if a stranger 'whose character is in doubt'. Boswell uses his diary as literary portraiture to set the record straight. On 7 April 1779, he records that Johnson disliked being reminded that Boswell often had a headache after drinking with him.

> [Johnson] 'Nay, Sir, it was not the *wine* that had your head ache but the *sense* I put into it.'
> [Boswell] 'Well, Sir, will sense make the head ache?'
> [Johnson] 'Yes, Sir, when it is not used to it.'

As a biographer in training, Boswell declares in his *London Journal* that he intends to use 'the sallies of my luxuriant imagination' to profit his writing by recording 'the anecdotes and the stories that I hear'. In 1764–6, while touring Germany and Switzerland, he reflects on his journal, 'Does it not contain a faithful register of my variations of mind? Does it not contain many ingenious observations and pleasing strokes which can afterwards be enlarged? Well, but I may die. True, I may live, and what rich treasure for my after days will be this my journal.' Both his *London Journal* and *Journal of a Tour to the Hebrides* chart his literary apprenticeship under Johnson's mentoring that in 1791 results in the English language's first great biography.

Yet three decades earlier, a stung Boswell refuted a friend's dig that 'he imagined that my journal did me harm, as it made me hunt about for adventures to adorn it with'. His friend, Temple, had missed the point. Boswell's own adventures were meant to equally command centre stage. He was hero and protagonist of his own journal. 'I wished to contain a consistent picture of a young fellow eagerly pushing his way through life.' The professional diarist had arrived. 'The greatness of his life was open,' Robert Louis Stevenson noted of Pepys, 'yet he longed to communicate its smallness also.' That shifts with Boswell. 'I find I journalise too tediously. Let me try to abbreviate.' Casting his lot with ambition writ large, he notes, 'Men are wise in proportion, not to their experience, but to their capacity for experience.'

And so from brilliant amateur Pepys to professional Boswell, the diary – this Book of the Self – is forever open to tweaking, rewriting, polishing. Not only its pages but the persona emerging from them. With light-year speed Boswell sets diaries on a straight course, anticipating the twenty-first-century blogger to whom he gives his own licence: 'I should live no more than I can record.'

Ninth – Twentieth Century:
Travel and Explorer Diaries

It is a strange thing that in sea voyages, where there is nothing to be seen but sky and sea, men should make diaries, but in land travel, wherein so much is to be observed, for the most part they omit it; as if chance were fitter to be registered than observation. Let diaries therefore be brought in use.

– Francis Bacon, *Of Travel*

In AD 809, Li Ao, a Chinese scholar and traveller, stopped in Kung to write.

8 February: 'I fell ill from the cold and drank scallion wine to sweat out the fever.'

16 February: 'My illness grew more acute, requiring a doctor to examine my pulse. Sent a servant to summon a physician.'

20 February: 'I slowly recovered from my illness.'

In between writing those entries, he travelled down three torrential rivers and spent sleepless nights in four outposts in rural central China. Li Ao would travel 2,500 miles in six months, the last stop in exile in remote Kuang Prefecture. By the time he arrived in southern China, he'd leave the world's first surviving travel diary, *Diary of My Coming to the South*.

While fragments of earlier travel accounts exist – the Bordeaux Pilgrim left the first Christian travel account of the Holy Land in AD 333 – Li Ao's diary anticipates the flurry of travel logs and journals that had their true origins in the eleventh and twelfth centuries. The boom in personal travel accounts marked the sharp rise in pilgrimages; thousands of European pilgrims set out annually for Jerusalem. As they boarded ships in Venice or Bari, private citizens soon discovered what Marcus Aurelius had on his military campaign: travel proved the ideal spur to self-reflective writing. Like Aurelius' *Meditations*, the earliest travel accounts are motivated by moral self-improvement. By the twelfth century, visiting holy shrines had become a focal point for motivating the inner life. And with that, travel and first-person accounts became forever linked.

What marks a historic step in Li Ao's AD 809 account is that a travel journal not only had a purpose – in Li Ao's case, mapping travel routes – but also, as significantly, an audience. His diary was written for fellow colleagues in Kuang. By the twelfth and thirteenth century, the pilgrim diary would also claim this dual purpose. English pilgrims, having the long travel distance to the Holy Land, kept personal accounts for those at home who couldn't travel – or read. Often a diary was dedicated to those sponsoring the journey.

What can be considered a travel journal? Captain Cook's ship logs? Letters explorers such as Columbus sent home that were subsequently collected? Scrolls Japanese pilgrims had stamped at temples and then hung at home upon their return? Or the fourteen-foot rolled vellum scrolls mapping holy sites visited by their Christian counterparts? As early as AD 381–4, Egeria, a Gallic female pilgrim, left her mark in a travel journal written as an ongoing letter intended for a circle of women at home. The hardships and dangers of early Christian and medieval travel doomed countless journals. Those that survive set the standard for all future travel journals: in undertaking perilous voyages, the ratio of physical difficulty mirrored the magnitude of inner struggle to be overcome.

If the pilgrim is the forerunner of the modern traveller, then journals are the inevitable aide, as indispensable as maps. Many of the first travel guides relied heavily on first-hand pilgrim accounts, often copied and embellished by later hands. In his *Itinerarium Antioni Placentina*, Antoninus, the Piacenza pilgrim, travelled to Jerusalem in the 570s, making notes on Sinai and Elias' cave. His guilty notations could easily be found in any modern travel diary. While venerating holy shrines, he can't resist the temptation to compromise them. In Cana, he reclines on what he's assured is the sacred marriage couch. He confesses, 'and there, unworthy that I was, I wrote the names of my parents'.

Some of the world's earliest diaries are in Arabic – Ibn Banna's eleventh-century diary is the first to order diary entries by date. It's not surprising then that the Islamic medieval culture that revolutionised mathematics and science should also innovate a new stage in first-person travel accounts: combining pilgrimage with scientific expedition. One such Islamic scholar traveller might be credited with the earliest oral diary. Ibn Battuta was the Muslim world's Marco Polo. In 1325 he set out on pilgrimage to Mecca, returning to Tangier only twenty-nine years later. He covered 75,000 miles, travelling the full sweep of the Mediterranean to Turkey and Egypt, and later into India and China. He took all forms of transport, but mostly travelled on foot or by caravan. Like his Christian pilgrim counterparts, he visited shrines and relics to spur introspection. 'I set out alone, having neither fellow-traveller in whose companionship I might find cheer, nor caravan whose party I might join, but swayed by an overwhelming impulse within me.' Without complaint, he records surviving the Great Plague in Damascus in 1348; having to wear three fur coats and two sets of woollen boots in wintry Turkey; noting his feet are so swollen by desert heat that blood darkens under his toenails.

Throughout his 75,000 miles, Ibn Battuta reports miracles, visits living saints and venerates mosque tombs. He also worships food and hospitality. The Sultan of Maqdashaw's servants greet him with platters of betel and areca nuts and jugs of rosewater; they cook unripe bananas in milk; scatter pickled lemons over chicken. In India peasants live on peas and turmeric-roasted lizards; in Granada, on fried beef and calabash with curdled milk. He lodges with merchants and sultans, records a multitude of languages and studies customs. Among his encounters, he meets the Byzantine Emperor, sees an asteroid, buys a Greek slave girl at Ephesus for forty dinars, views the Pyramids, marries ten women en route.

Travel sharpened Ibn Battuta's keen instinct for both adventure and social observation. In India, he notes aphrodisiac pills a yogi had concocted for the Sultan of Madurai. 'Among their ingredients were iron filings, and the Sultan was so pleased with their effect that he took an overdose and died.' He notices tiny metal rings on women's hems for servants to lift so as not to muddy fabric. Weary from travel, he still manages to record the strange. In February 1351 his caravan reached Taghaza, in Mali. Situated on a dry salt lake, all the buildings were constructed from slabs of salt quarried by slaves of the Masufa tribe. From the mines, the 200-pound blocks were transported to Timbuktu and swapped for gold. 'After twenty-five days we reached Taghaza, an unattractive village with the curious feature that its houses and mosques are built of blocks of salt, roofed with camel skins. There are no trees there. Nothing but sand.' Waylaid in the desert, he rues: 'We passed ten days of discomfort there, because the water is brackish and the place is plagued by flies... Truffles are plentiful in this desert and it swarms with lice, so that people wear string necklaces containing mercury, which kills them.'

On Ibn Battuta's return home in 1354, the Sultan of Morocco commissioned his travels be recorded for posterity. As the son of a legal scholar, Ibn Battuta had a prodigious memory, fortified by repeating his stories in new countries. He dictated his travel memories to a young scribe, Ibn Juzayy. The first oral travel journal stretched into four volumes. Ibn Battuta produced the world's longest travel account: *A Gift to Those Who Contemplate the Wonders of Cities and the Marvels of Travelling*.

Ibn Battuta had travelled the sweep of the known Islamic world, chronicling its shrines and sites. Felix Fabri, a Dominican pilgrim, writes of his embarrassment at his fellow Christians' bad manners. 'I say of a truth, that in forty weeks of this pilgrimage, a man learns to know himself better than in forty years elsewhere. I confess that I never saw my own shortcomings and vices better or more clearly than during these my wanderings.' In 1483 he set out from Ulm for Mount Sinai's St Catherine Monastery. *The Wanderings of Felix Fabri* is a two-volume medieval Michelin Guide, offering church updates and accommodation tips. His is the first to offer sections on travel etiquette. Felix Fabri lays out rules for knights charged with protecting pilgrims, as well as pointers for travellers to respect the cultures they're visiting.

'Alas! My kind brethren, in order that I may tell you of this, I am forced to change my style, and must offer to you to drink the cup of bitterness which I myself have mournfully received.' He records sharing tents with knights and pilgrim travellers, finding dung in his boots and shaking them out every morning. He finds the conditions inside shrines as hazardous as on the road. Of the Holy Sepulchre, he laments, 'During my first pilgrimage, the roof of the church, which is of great weight because it is made of lead, was threatening to fall upon the choir.' He saves his despair for fellow Christians' behaviour – pilgrims eating rather than fasting in churches, taking stones from walls for souvenirs, flocking to peddlers hawking supposed holy relics. Visiting the Church of Bethlehem, he rues: 'I loathe to speak of this event, but the ruin and piteous contempt into which the place has fallen, and which must be wept for.'

Sir Richard Torkington's 1516–17 travel diary to Jerusalem boasts of being *Ye Oldest Diarie of Englysshe Travell*. Torkington, a pilgrim priest, had met with Anne Boleyn's father in Norfolk before the trip. 'We were out of England in our said pilgrimage the space of an whole year, five weeks, and three days,' he wrote on 17 April 1518. Torkington had set out from Rye, Sussex, travelled to Rome and then on to Jerusalem. Travel took him from Italy, to Rhodes, Cyprus and the Holy Land. In his diaries we see what still plagues the modern travel diary: the impossible expectations, the anxiety of surviving a journey, the hope of being transformed by it. His struggles with the inner life are as perilous as the pilgrimage he's made to overcome them. In Torkington's hands, the diary is an ideal place to record – and complain. Reaching Italy, after much discomfort, he's reassured by the twenty-three new ships being constructed to take pilgrims like himself to Jerusalem.

His travel diary shows that pilgrimage offered more worldly temptations than absolution from them. In Venice, Torkington writes about forgetting saints' names but delighting over tables heavy with silver dishes. An entry impatiently records having to wait his turn during an eight-course dinner for the Venetian doge. Less the penitent pilgrim than the traveller owed his due, he concedes, 'And when dinner was done, the Duke [doge] sent to the pilgrims great basins full of marchpanes, and also comfits and malmsey, and other sweet wine, as much as any man would eat and drink.' The emporium of Venetian pleasures is recorded in far greater detail than any shrine. He's spellbound by dancers 'disguised in women's clothes... tumblers, both men and children, the most marvellous fellows I ever saw, so much that I cannot write it'.

In his travel diary, grand expectations and shoddy lodgings are duly noted. As his ship anchored, 'at Jaffa beginith the holy land; at this haven Jonas the prophet took the sea'. Soon he's less the humble pilgrim and more the irritated traveller. Once landed, they 'were received by Turks and Saracens, and put into an old cave by name and tale'. Like any waylaid traveller, he complains, 'we lay in the same grot or cave all night upon the stinking stable ground, as well night as day, right evil entreated by the said

Turkish moors.' Finally, he is taken up Mount Sinai. Later, as if to atone for churlishness, he records, 'We went to the house where the sins of Mary Magdalen were forgiven.'

A new form of travel diary surfaces by the late sixteenth century. Thomas Dallam is a diarist on another kind of pilgrimage, less to improve the self than trade. Thomas Dallam was a Lancashire-born organ builder. While he later built organs for King's College, Cambridge, and Worcester Cathedral, in 1599 he journeyed to Turkey to present the sultan with a new organ commissioned by Queen Elizabeth. The trip was to fortify an alliance with Sultan Mohammed III against the Spanish, necessary to the trade commissions carried out by the Levant Company. Dallam's mission was unique: to transport an intricate mechanical clock organ, 'a great and curious present is going to the Grand Turk, which will scandalise other nations'. In Dallam's travel diary, cross and crescent unite for commerce.

'In this Book is the Account of an Organ Carryed to the Grand Seignor and Other Curious Matter.' At the start of his travel diary Dallam records: 'Necessities for my voyage to Turkey, the which I brought upon a very short warning, having no friend to advise me in any things.' Like any harried traveller, he uses the diary's first page to make a two-page inventory of what he'll need – flannel waistcoats, hats, handkerchiefs, britches, garters, gloves, knives, a sword, nutmeg, oil, cloves, sugar and, of course, prunes. In 1599 he sailed on the *Hector*, travelling to Rhodes, Damascus and Aleppo. On arriving in Constantinople, he notes, 'when we opened our chests we found that all gluing work was clean decayed, by reason that it had lain above six months in the hold of our ship, with the workings of the sea and the hotness of the country.'

While Dallam chronicles the organ's lengthy repair, his diary offers glimpses inside the Ottoman Empire's iron-door palaces with their forbidden harems. The sultan and his mother arrive in a golden boat to inspect the *Hector*. When Dallam finally enters the many-gated, marble-columned palace, 'the Grand Sinyor, having a desire to see his present, came hither with marvellous great speed'. The sultan sat as the present from Queen Elizabeth was unveiled: a sixteen-foot organ with a portrait of the queen surrounded by forty-five diamonds, rubies and emeralds. The organ could play for six hours at a stretch. Its clock struck twenty-two times, followed by sixteen bells chiming. 'Then the music went off, and the organ played a song of five parts.' As the music finished, on top of the organ a holly bush full of automated blackbirds and thrushes shook their mechanical wings. 'Then the Grand Sinyor sayed it was good.'

'The great Oriental Traveller', Dr John Covel, kept diaries long before returning to become vice-chancellor of Cambridge University. In 1670 he travelled to Constantinople as chaplain to the English Ambassador and to the Levant Company. A scientist and clergyman, Covel travelled extensively in Asia Minor between 1670 and 1679. He intended his diary for publication, dividing it into chapters and inserting relevant illustrations. It languished in the British Museum until 1893 when the Hakluyt Society gave Covel his wish. But only reluctantly. In its preface they noted, 'It is easy to see why any publisher would recoil from bringing out so prolix a work for the Doctor is wearisome in the extreme.' A long 'dissertation' on his seasickness fills pages, while his accounts of Carthage or Ephesus catalogue every monument and stone. While of historic interest, Covel's travel journals lack the self-reflection of the earliest pilgrim diaries. Travel had improved trade but not the eye of the recorder.

What makes a great travel diary or journal? It takes us where we will probably never go: the top of Everest, the tip of Tierra del Fuego, the frozen reaches of Antarctica. Its entries contain a clear storyline of man exploring and battling the elements. The best travel diaries involve human nature played out in physical locations designed to test it. Some, such as Captain Cook's, show that even in the most exotic landscape one thing remains constant: human nature. Cook made his first voyage around the world in 1768–71; the second in 1776. His travel notes show that it's possible to travel around the globe but never leave complaints far behind. He rues,

> Such are the tempers and dispositions of seamen in general that whatever you give them out of the common way – altho' it be ever so much for their good – it will not go down and you will hear nothing but murmurings against the man who first invented it; but the moment they see their superiors set a value upon it, it becomes the finest stuff in the world and the inventor an honest fellow. Wind easterly.

By the late eighteenth century, travel diaries such as Boswell's *Journal of a Tour of Corsica* absorb the richness of the foreign landscapes that they chronicle. Just as the appetite for silk and spices had linked and extended trade routes, so the quest to travel far beyond them beckoned Grand Tour diarists. Travel had liberated the recording eye. Travel journals soon recorded something larger than an individual consciousness – its global reach. If English Puritan and Quaker diaries started in service of mapping the inner life, early nineteenth-century travel diaries record mapping actual frontiers. Undiscovered terrains, rather than ancient and sacred places, were now the fixation of the most important travel diaries. Utopia was the travel diarist's destination.

On 31 August 1803, Lewis and Clark and eleven others started out on the first American transcontinental expedition to the Pacific Northwest. Thomas Jefferson had charged naturalists Meriwether Lewis and William Clark with finding a water passage across the North American continent. Travel journals were obligatory. The explorers traversed what, in time, became ten American states, travelling 8,000 miles in two and a half years. Exploring the vast stretch between the Missouri River and the Pacific Ocean, they minutely recorded what until then had only been seen by Native American eyes. Midway, in North Dakota, Sacagawea, a Shoshone female translator and guide, joined their Corps of Discovery.

The journals, later published in thirteen volumes, are comprised of field notebooks, open or public journals, as well as those kept for the explorers themselves. The two explorers wrote 'afloat and ashore, legibly and illegibly, and always with an urgent sense of purpose'. Both journal keepers, but especially Lewis, left journals prized by naturalists, geologists and anthropologists. By the time they returned across the Continental Divide in 1806, the journals contained the vast inventory of botanical specimens, maps, and geological information that allowed the government to claim land, including the Louisiana Purchase.

Lewis and Clark are the Pepys of the natural world. Driven by intense curiosity, they filled hundreds of journal pages, often carrying small notebooks in their pockets. In July 1804 Clark wrote:

> I observed artificial mounds (or as I may more justly term graves) which to me is strong evidence of this country being once thickly settled. (The Indians of the Missouri's still keep up the custom of burying their dead on high ground)... Gathered some grapes, really ripe. On a sandstone bluff about a quarter of a mile from its mouth on the lower side, I observed some Indian marks. Went to the rock which jutted over the water and marked my name and the day of the month and year.

That habit provided generations of future trekkers with destinations like Pompey's Pillar in Montana simply by following the Clark's travel coordinates. After carving his initials in the rock, Clark snaps back to the immediate world of duty. The same entry continues: 'Tried a man for sleeping at his post, and inspected the arms, ammunition, etc., of the party. Found all complete. Took some lunar observations. Three deer killed today.

Latitude 39° 55′ 56′ N.'

Their travel journals provided the first systematic meteorological record of continental America. Just as they catalogued varieties of thunderstorms, Lewis and Clark noted 100 new species of animals and 176 unknown plants and wildflowers. As diarists, they switched between naturalists and budding anthropologists. A sizeable portion of the journals detail the fifty Indian tribes Jefferson instructed them to meet, including Sioux, Lakota and Nez Perce. Six linguistic families are noted; two-column headings for tribal names and their translation: Iron Eyes, the Big Horse, Crow's Head. An entry records a snub – a greeting Indian tribal party that hadn't sent the chief elders. Like travellers introduced to strange food, the diarists record it immediately – roasted corn, buffalo tongue, dried salmon. On 26 September 180, Lewis records Indian faces painted with coal, bodies greased with animal fat, hawk feathers and porcupine quills worn as headdresses. Clark then visits the same tribe: 'I was received on an elegant painted buffalo robe, and taken to the village by six men, and was not permitted to touch the ground until I was later put down in the grand council home, on a white dressed robe.'

Their travel diaries offer a cinematic glimpse of a world of both bewildering wild abundance and seasonal scarcity. Entries record buffalo so emaciated only the tongues could be eaten. At the Pacific, they boil seawater for salt, collecting twelve gallons for the journey back. The power of Lewis and Clark's journals is a world as first glimpsed, played off against the heartbreak of all that's now vanished – 3,000 buffalo, herds of antelope and elk, rivers teeming with freshwater fish.

Transatlantic travel was considerably safer by 1831, the year Charles Darwin set out on a nearly five-year voyage around the world. Trained in medicine and divinity, he joined the survey voyage as an unpaid naturalist. On 27 December 1831, the twenty-five-year-old Darwin brought with him fifteen note-books to record the new specimens he was charged with collecting and studying. As he boarded HMS *Beagle*, his work as a naturalist would later be defined by notebooks that 'determined my whole career'. The specimens he collected, particularly those gathered off the coasts of South America, provided the research out of which he formulated his theory of evolution and natural selection. The notebooks proved instrumental for his 1859 *The Origin of Species.*

Darwin's explorer notebooks have been called 'travel memoir and science primer'. His notebooks were inspired by Bacon's maxim that reading makes 'a full man', but writing 'an exact one'. During his travels, Darwin filled 2,070 pages with 116,080 words in fifteen pocket notebooks and other journals. The majority of the longer entries were written during the middle voyage years. As the *Beagle* charted coastlines off South America, Darwin was on land surveying and collecting specimens. His 1831–6 notebooks were divided into field notebooks, specimen catalogues and zoological diaries. The field notebooks are a jumble of records, from notes on South American Indians to his reading lists and financial calculations. Soon he learned to balance a notebook against the rocks he was studying. 'By placing a notebook on it, the measurement can be made very accurately.'

Darwin's pencil-jotted entries are written in a natural style. On 6 December 1834 the *Beagle* dropped anchor off the island of San Pedro. 'A fox (*Canis fulvipes*) of a kind said to be peculiar to the island, and very rare in it, and, which is a new species, was sitting on the rocks. He was so intently absorbed in watching the work of the officers that I was able, by quietly walking up behind, to knock him on the head with my geological hammer.' Beyond a naturalist's fervent interest in the immediate world, the notebooks reveal Darwin's larger curiosity about its operating principle. Lewis and Clark's had noted antelope, wild turkeys and buffalo fattening on acorns. Darwin used his notebooks to underline that fierce struggle implied in those notations: the survival of the fittest. Lewis and Clark catalogued species. Darwin transformed the world's view of the origins of those species.

As a naturalist, Darwin also had a keen anthropological eye. His notebooks contain deftly drawn portraits of tribes he met on his travels. On 19 November 1833 he spent a night on an Argentine estate near the Rio Negro. Of the locals he observes,

They expressed, as was usual, unbounded astonishment at the globe being round, and could scarcely credit that a hole would, if deep enough, come out on the other side. They had, however, heard of a country where there were six months of light and six of darkness... They were curious about the price and conditions of horses and cattle in England. Upon finding out we did not catch our animals with the lazo, they cried out, 'Ah, then, you use nothing but the bolas': the idea of an enclosed country was quite new to them.

Darwin's notebooks record linguistics in the New World. In an entry for 17 December 1832, he writes of the quick mimicking intelligence of tribal elders on Tierra del Fuego. To communicate friendship, an elder observes the party 'patting our breasts and making a chuckling kind of noise, as people do when feeding chickens'. The tribe responds with impeccable manners.

They are excellent mimics as often as we coughed or yawned or made any odd motion, they immediately imitated us... They could repeat with perfect correctness each words in any sentence we addressed them, and they remembered such words for some time. Yet we Europeans all know how difficult it is to distinguish apart sounds in a foreign language. Which of us, for instance, could follow an American Indian through a sentence of more than three words?

Towards the end of the *Beagle* voyage, Darwin started making notes in the now-labelled Red Notebook. He used it to begin formulating his thoughts on evolution. On his return to London in 1836, Darwin combed through his fifteen notebooks and started rewriting his journal. Over the next decade, he kept coming back to his multiple entries on mockingbirds and finches studied off the Galapagos. He realised they were in fact different species from those seen in Chile. His fifteen notebooks stand in similar magnitude with Galileo's surviving notebooks.

Scottish explorer and missionary David Livingstone kept journals while travelling deep into the central and southern interior of Africa. The first European to cross the width of southern Africa between 1852–6, Livingstone wrote detailed entries on newly charted geography, its peoples and customs – a fascination of his since his earliest expeditions to discover the Nile's sources. Livingstone's journals ranged from his daily Letts diary to pocket notebooks to scraps of paper torn from old magazines. His journals span three different expedition stages – 1852–6, 1852–64 and 1866–74. They proved invaluable memory prompts for his bestselling 1857 *Missionary Travels in South Africa* and his 1865 *Zambesi and its Tributaries*, the latter chronicling the doomed 1858–64 Zambezi River Expedition in the service of 'Christianity, Commerce and Civilisation'.

While he was the first European to see and re-name Victoria Falls, his journals record more struggle and tested faith with each expedition. On 27 April 1862, he notes his wife Mary's unexpected death at Shupanga. She'd just joined him in his second journey and was taken suddenly by fever. 'I said to her a few days before her fatal illness, "We bodies ought to be more sober and not play so much."' After her death, he imagined his own grave 'in some far-off, still, deep forest where I may sleep sweetly till the resurrection morn'. The later journals record the arduous ten years before that would happen. For six years Livingstone virtually lost contact with the outside world. Instead, his diaries record arduous treks through swamps, enduring cholera or pneumonia after weeks of unrelenting rain. Thirty journal entries alone are devoted to him having to halt treks because of illness.

Livingstone was the first European to see Zambia's Lake Bangweulu. He returned in April 1873, arriving in the village of Illala with ulcerated feet and a left arm weakened after a lion attack. The journal records symptoms of malaria. Disoriented by fever, gaunt from dysentery, pale from blood loss, he found a pencil and wrote in his journal, 'It is not all pleasure this exploration.' Livingstone died on 1 May 1873, his body – and diaries – carried a thousand miles to the coast by his two native servants. The final pages of his journal are blank. If his faithful caretakers had known how to write, they would have recorded that his heart was buried under a Mulva tree where he'd died.

In their journals, Captain Cook, Lewis and Clark and Darwin all note ship latitudes and coordinates. In a deeper sense, their journals reflect a way to orient themselves in unfamiliar worlds. Beyond dangerous voyages or expeditions, the timeless appeal of such journals is the diarist's courage to act on an initial curiosity. By the mid-nineteenth century, expedition travel was no longer the goal of explorers but of ordinary citizens. Lewis and Clark had sought a passageway across America's rivers, but overland travel wasn't much easier a half century later. The steady recording hand and unflinching gaze of the diarist is most evident in American pioneer diaries. In search of free land before and after the 1849 California Gold Rush, pioneers took their diaries with them in wagons, on horseback and on foot.

Western pioneer travel diaries record the dangers both in nature and in human nature. In 1846 twelve-year-old Narcissa Cornwall noted in her diary: 'Father was busy reading and did not notice that the house was being filled with strange Indians until Mother spoke about it.' Her father, a Presbyterian minister, was migrating westward to free land in California. The family made it safely across the Plains to Oregon. Less fortunate were several families that left sets of travel diaries. Their pages reveal a dark twist on Darwin's theory of survival of the fittest – an 1846 travel expedition gone tragically wrong.

The Donner Party, a group of westward-bound travellers, set out in covered wagons to make the 2,500-mile trek from Illinois to California. Families joined en route, including Irish-born Patrick Breen. On 5 April 1846 he set out with his wife and seven children. He'd made his own diary for the trip, folding and trimming eight sheets of letter paper into a thirty-two-page journal. Towards the end of the overland trip only three pages remained blank. That blankness marks one of the most harrowing incidents in the history of travel journals.

While many of their diaries survive, of the eighty-three original Donner Party members, only forty-five reached California. In the winter of 1846, they made the ill-fated decision to cross the Sierra Nevadas. Low on supplies, the families set up camps to wait out an onslaught of blizzards. One child in the camps was George Donner's youngest daughter, Eliza.

> After the first storm, for the snow bank in front of the cabin door was not high enough to keep out a little sunbeam that stole down the steps and make a bright spot upon our floor. I saw it, and sat down under it, held it on my lap, passed my hand up and down its brightness, and found that I could break its ray in two… Finally I gathered up a piece of it in my apron and ran to my mother. Great was my surprise when I carefully opened the folds and found I had nothing to show.

It wasn't a sunbeam that was breaking apart but the Donner Party itself. Within months, her parents perished. Patrick Breen's diary notes the constant snow, the growing starvation. In mid-December, fifteen others set out on snowshoes, quickly trapped by blizzard without shelter. When four died, the others survived by cannibalism to make their way to safety. In 1847, Eliza and her sister were rescued by the third relief party. In 1911, sixty-four years later, she used many of the diaries, including Patrick Breen's, and published *The Expedition of the Donner Party and Its Tragic Fate*.

'Night. Height 10,530 ft. Temp -16.3°F. Minimum -25.8°F. Another hard grind in the afternoon and five miles added. About seventy-four miles from the Pole – can we keep this up for seven days?' In his entry for 11 January 1912, Captain Robert Falcon Scott was within reach of the South Pole. Two years into his second Antarctic expedition, Scott's Terra Nova Expedition hoped to surpass his 1900–4 Discovery Expedition. On 17 January the moment of glory sours for Scott and his remaining four companions. 'The worst has happened,' he records after noticing 'a black speck ahead'. It's a flag. Seeing it and fresh ski tracks, Scott knows the Norwegians had reached the Pole first. In the next day's entry, after noting coordinates, he simply writes, 'The Pole.' As the bitter realisation sinks in, he adds, 'Great God! This is an awful place.'

Scott's explorer diary is the most hauntingly dramatic of any travel journal; most of its entries are framed by precise coordinates as his party braves a frozen hell on their 800-mile journey back towards safety. His journal rivets despite our already knowing what's in store for Scott and his party. The stoic clarity of Scott's entries and the harrowing details they record sustain the journal's unrelieved tension. As the expedition begins its long descent, the explorers are already short on rations and far from the nearest depot. One by one, Scott records his party succumbing to nightmarish conditions. Blizzards, snow blindness, frostbite. On 17 February a frostbitten, disoriented Edgar Evans is 'broken down in the brain', after falls on the glacier. He dies that same day. By 11 March Scott writes with scientific disinterest, taking an inventory of items required if they need to end lives – thirty opium tablets each, a tube of morphine between them.

On 17 March 1912 Scott starts his journal entry with no coordinates. He wonders if he's lost track of dates, but he correctly dates it 17 March. In the diary's final entries, he is already recording for the inevitable end. Scott's instinct for precision and clarity is both heartbreaking and unnerving. 'Should this be found I want these facts recorded,' he writes. He records dutifully that Titus Oates' last thought was of his mother, and that before dying Oates had imagined his old regiment being proud of so heroic a death, suffering met with courage.

Scott's final entries for 21–29 March are kept with stoic dignity. By 21 March, the party is within eleven miles of the nearest depot. Low on fuel, they're down to two items of food. On 23

March he notes, 'have decided it shall be natural' – as an explorer, he will die in his tracks. Aware of his fate, in his journal he's still noting wind direction, calculating two cups of tea apiece as a new blizzard swirls outside the tent. 'I do not think we can hope for any better things now. We shall stick it out to the end, but we are getting weaker of course, and the end cannot be far. It seems a pity, but I do not think I can write more.' On 29 March, he managed the journal's final seven words: 'For god's sake look after our people.' The search party arrived on 12 November 1912, finding the Terra Nova Expedition bodies and Scott's diaries.

Imagining the trip he'd soon make deep into the birch-dense New England woods, Henry David Thoreau wrote, 'When I go out for an evening, I arrange the fire in my stove so that I do not fail to find a good one when I return... And this is the art of living, too – to leave our life in a condition to go alone.' The entry is from one of the world's most singular travel journals. Throughout his life, Henry David Thoreau voraciously read first-hand world travel accounts and was later obsessed with Darwin's *Voyage of the Beagle*. Unlike his neighbour and friend, the epic traveller and diarist Ralph Waldo Emerson, Thoreau intended to keep a different travel journal. In his, he'd journey widely while not going far from home. Between 1837–61, he filled thirty-nine notebooks with two million words. Thoreau's journals, kept during his two-year experiment to 'live deliberately', produced his classic, *Walden*, forever changing the inward traveller.

On 4 July 1845 Thoreau travelled to Walden Pond, a mile and a half from the centre of Concord, Massachusetts. The New England town was home to diarists Emerson, Margaret Fuller and the Alcotts, and the birthplace of Transcendentalism.

With journals in hand, Thoreau began his two-year experiment in far-reaching travel. His goal was to achieve what travellers left home to do: to see their own world more clearly. In exchange for clearing woods on land Emerson owned, he built a 'tightly shingled and plastered' small cottage on the edge of Walden Pond, ideal for a poet philosopher with a practical bent.

Thoreau was also a surveyor and naturalist. Between 1845–7, Walden was his experiment in simple living and sustained conscious observation. By living in, and recording, nature, Thoreau used his journals 'to see if I could not learn what it had to teach, and not, when I came to die, discover that I had not lived'.

At Walden, Thoreau perfected the inward travel journal. He tore off birch bark as he walked around Walden Pond, jotting down ideas with pencils he'd made. The seed for his experiment had long been in his journals. As early as 2 December 1839, he argued that a contemplative life was worth more than a 'whole campaign of daring'. As a journal keeper, he likened himself to a clerk in a counting room, making an evening transfer of notations from daybook into ledger. A tireless walker, Thoreau often stalked the tracks of earlier Indian settlers, making original and precise observations of nature that set the standard for modern nature writing.

Between 4 July 1845 and 6 September 1847, Thoreau's Walden journals defined those he would keep for the rest of his life. They transformed from a notational diary to a writer's notebook to the source for his poetry, essays and books. Fourteen of his twenty volumes of writing would be his journals. At Walden, he drafted *A Week on the Concord and Merrimack Rivers* (1849) and formulated *Walden* (1854). 'The frontiers are not east or west, north or south, but wherever a man "fronts" a fact,' he wrote at Walden, beginning to work on his famous essay 'On Civil Disobedience'. 'Nay, be a Columbus to whole new continents and worlds within you, opening new channels, not of trade, but of thought.' Like Darwin's notebooks, Thoreau's journals revolutionised modern thought. His essay, 'On Civil Disobedience', on conscientious objection and social justice, directly influenced Tolstoy, Gandhi and Martin Luther King. His and Emerson's own ten published volumes of diaries gave birth to Transcendentalism, based on self-reliance and conscious living. In Thoreau's Walden journals, environmentalists first found their true source of inspiration.

In 1860, two years before he died, Thoreau wrote that any fool can make a rule and any fool will mind it. Independent travellers ever since have been guided by an entry he made on 21 July 1851.

I see the track of a bare human foot in the dusty road, the toes and muscles all faithfully imprinted. Such a sight is so rare that it affects me with surprise, as the footprint of Juan Fernandez did Crusoe. It is equally rare here. I am affected as if some Indian or South-Sea-Islander had been along, some man who had a foot. I am slow to be convinced that any of my neighbors – the judge on the bench, the parson in the pulpit – might have made that... It is pleasant as it is to see the tracks of cows and deer and birds. I am brought so much nearer to the tracker – when again I think of the sole of my own foot – that when I behold that of his shoe merely, or am introduced to him and converse with him in the usual way, I am disposed to say to the judge whom I meet, 'Make tracks.'

Eighteenth – Twentieth Century: Writers, Artists, Creative Diaries

Jan. 16. Read – wrote – fired pistols – returned – wrote – visited – heard music – talked nonsense – and went home. Wrote part of a Tragedy – advanced in Act I with 'all deliberate speed.' Bought a blanket.

– Byron, Diary, 1816

'Do you really keep a diary?' Algernon asks Cecily in Oscar Wilde's *The Importance of Being Earnest*. 'I'd give anything to look at it. May I?' 'Oh, no,' she replies, covering it with her hand. 'You see, it is simply a very young girl's record of her own thoughts and impressions, and consequently meant for publication. When it appears in volume form I hope you will order a copy.'

When Wilde's play debuted in London's St James's Theatre on 14 February 1895, the audience roared at this scene. The laughter was self-knowing. The scene mocked the idealised diary keeper. Pensive, ruminative. Productive. For many in the audience, a leather diary was merely a stage prop on their desk. Wilde's own diary was often blank. But he was fascinated by diaries, subtitling his final play about them, 'A Trivial Comedy for Serious People'. The secret worth uncovering in Cecily's diary wasn't only the habit of successful journal keeping. Wilde had hit upon the connection between a diary and the larger creative work that often came directly out of it. Tantalizingly, Cecily disguises that hard effort much as Wilde spent months polishing his bright spontaneous banter.

Since the late eighteenth century, writers' diaries have served as sketchpad and storehouse. Journals and notebooks have been an auxiliary part of creative process. Stendhal kept reading lists, Hugo jotted conversation for dialogue, Scott brooded on revision, Kafka noted dreams, and Gide observed the psyche's split between private creator and public persona. 'I am happy to be both halves, the watcher and the watched,' Camus observed in his notebooks. Writers have left a long working record of creative process and habits, as varied as the journals themselves – from Dostoyevsky's three memoranda diaries while composing *Crime and Punishment* to Camus' *cashiers* notebooks while drafting *The Stranger*, 'put fragments of diary (ending) at the beginning of the novel'. However varied in form, the best diaries have a common trait. They allow us to eavesdrop on a writer in process. From Byron to Graham Greene, we watch them negotiating the obstacle course of creative life – bad nights, false starts, idleness, fame.

'Lev brought me a file containing *The Death of Ivan Ilyich* for the new edition. Then he took it away again, and published an announcement saying he would make it public property,' Sonya Tolstoy wrote in her diary on 15 February 1895. 'Fulfilling a promise to S. I read through all my journals for the past seven years,' Leo Tolstoy wrote in his. Sonya's entry was made the night after Wilde's play debuted. The Tolstoys were living its most famous scene first hand. No couple tells us more about the complex role a diary plays in creative life than Tolstoy and his wife. In the Tolstoys' dual set of diaries we see the entire arc of creative life: from the first seeds of inspiration for novels, to the struggle of literary creation – writing, editing, endless rewriting – from literary censorship to publishing, royalties, literary rights and estate executors.

From courtship in 1862 to Tolstoy's death in 1910, their lives were defined by diaries. A year into marriage, Tolstoy decided they should share theirs. For forty-two years, they read, wrote in and commented on the other's diaries. Together, the diaries provide a four-decade portrait of ambition in a turbulent marriage divided over publication, ownership and copyright. As Tolstoy's earlier notational diaries shift to reflection, Sonya's turn epic, running some 800 pages. Almost every entry in the tandem diaries offers a look at life with – or as – a literary genius.

'Here is a fact which needs to be remembered more often,' Tolstoy wrote in his 1854 diary. 'Thackeray spent thirty years preparing to write his first novel. Alexandre Dumas writes two a week.' From the start, the Tolstoys' diaries record finding material for future projects and the ethics of using it. During their courtship, Tolstoy found a short story in Sonya's diary, a thinly veiled autobiographical account of three sisters all in love with the same man. 'What force of truth and simplicity,' he recorded that same night, 26 August 1862. The story's heroine, Natasha, and the sisters became the seed for the Rostov family in *War and Peace*. 'In his account of Levin's and Kitty's wedding,' Sonya wrote of his use of their own wedding in *Anna Karenina*, Tolstoy 'described the whole psychological process' – the groom's equivocation, the bride's weeping. The novel also used two incidents recorded in Sonya's diary: his proposing to her by chalking letters on a green felt billiard table; Tolstoy's handing her a stack of his bachelor diaries a day after his proposal.

The Tolstoys' diaries offer a rare portrait of the split between the creative and business sides of a writer's life. While Tolstoy's diary is sparse when writing his two masterpieces, Sonya's nearly doubles. By the late 1880s, seven sets of diaries, including several kept by the Tolstoy children, were recording within the household. Their son Ilya noted his father's habit of nightly leaving chapters crosshatched with corrections for Sonya to proof and copy. In manuscript, *War and Peace* ran to 3,000 pages. Sonya copied it six times. Tolstoy records Sonya moving from muse to copyist to copy editor. 'The whole historico-military side of *War and Peace*, over which I laboured so hard, was coming out badly,' he wrote, noting that Sonya advised 'that the best part would be the psychological side, the characters and the pictures of family life'.

Tolstoy's bachelor diaries detailing gambling, whoring, and siring a child on his estate had shocked Sonya. But she'd missed the diary's hidden agenda for self-improvement. In 1855 his diary forewarned, 'My career is literature – to write and write! From tomorrow I'll work all my life or throw up everything – rules, religion, propriety – everything.' From 1877–86, their diaries stake out opposing views of ambition after Tolstoy's spiritual crisis. 'Lev is working,' Sonya recorded, 'but alas! He keeps writing religious tracts until his head aches.' With his male secretary, Vladmir Chertkov, he started a publishing house. Sonya's diary records her planning and proofing editions. Tolstoy now shared his diaries with his newly installed publisher, whose moral causes were closer to his own. 'Although his last diaries are very interesting, they have all been *composed* for Chertkov and those who it pleases Mr Chertkov to show them,' Sonya complained in her diary on 7 July 1910. Three days later, *'go get the diaries back from Chertkov, all those little black oilcloth notebooks, and put them back on the desk, letting him have them one at a time, to make excerpts. That's all!'*

Sonya's jealousy, recorded in both diaries, showed a couple on a collision course. At stake was guardianship of the diaries. 'I've been reading through my books. I oughtn't to write any more,' Tolstoy reflected. 'I think in this respect, I've done all I could. But I want to, I terribly want to.' Tolstoy locked away his diaries. On 27 October 1910, after hearing Sonya 'searching, probably reading' the diaries in his study, the eighty-one-year-old Tolstoy left home. Three months earlier, Chertkov and Tolstoy's daughter Tanya had taken the ageing writer into a nearby forest where he'd signed all copyright over to them, making them the literary estate executors. Sonya's diary records Tolstoy dying in a remote railway station on 20 November 1910.

'You see for me – life and work are two things indivisible,' wrote Katherine Mansfield reflecting on leaving New Zealand for a literary career in London. A close friend of D.H. Lawrence and rival of Virginia Woolf, she had burned the 'huge, complaining' journals of childhood. In 1916 she started a new type of writer's journal after the death of her soldier brother. 'I want to keep a *minute notebook*, to be published one day.' The early stirrings of psychoanalysis and the explosion of interest in first-person accounts after World War I resulted in her using a journal to try out 'a kind of special prose'. Published posthumously in 1927, the journal became an instant bestseller. The interval leading to World War II was a tipping point for diaries. With the threat of war's isolation, a public was hungry for information not just about the connection between personal and creative life. It wanted what Mansfield's journal provided – a portrait of a writer struggling alone.

Why have some of the most widely read diaries, many still bestsellers, often been written by women? The exigencies of daily practical life and creative process are fused in a single diary. In Mansfield's, thumbnail sketches are followed by shopping lists, drafts of love letters, details for future stories. Who better to observe the obstacles – and hard-won solutions – to creative life than a diarist 'trained to silence', as Virginia Woolf said of herself. Since the late eighteenth century, diaries have been the missing link in creative life. Four diarists living in London from the eighteenth to the twentieth century show the arc of creative process in a writer's life. The diaries of Fanny Burney, Virginia Woolf, Katherine Mansfield and Sylvia Plath each offer a key to unlocking a crucial part of creativity: ambition, permission to use it, craft, voice. Diarists like Camus, Gide, Waugh and Greene reflect an already established literary career – writers grappling with the business of reviews, publishers and a network-rich social life. Centuries of literary prohibition and inhibition had driven women to diary keeping. Safe yet secret. The finest diaries expose the raw nerve of creative ambition. For writers like Mansfield and Woolf, by being able to practise craft, a diary became a first draft of confidence.

Before the public knew her as the witty, clever Fanny Burney, a celebrated fixture in Boswell's and Johnson's inner literary circle, she privately noted, 'I know that in journals, thoughts, actions, looks, conversations – *all* things go down; do they not?' Few diarists have moved faster from confession to craft than Fanny Burney. Four novels, eight plays, a biography, volumes of letters detailing London's literary and theatre life owe everything to the journal begun in 1768. The diaries, written in three stages over seventy-two years, show that process wasn't an easy one. By its final entries in 1839, her eight-volume diary had become a major literary work. More than any early journal keeper, hers shows the solitary diarist moving from private to public voice. At their core, Burney's diaries involve the deep permission to begin and sustain creative work.

Fanny Burney's journal is a fascinating look at a writer's life-long struggle to rid herself of a severe, carping, internalised critic. On 27 March 1768, fifteen-year-old Burney began a journal 'Addressed to a Certain Miss Nobody'. Burney's critical father strenuously discouraged her literary ambition. She invented an imaginary reader to free herself of crippling perfectionism. 'To Nobody then will I write my journal since to Nobody can I be wholly unreserved – to Nobody can I reveal every thought, every wish of my heart.' In the journal's opening entry, ambition for future novels is hidden in plain sight, 'To have some account of my thoughts, manners, acquaintance and action, when the hour arrives in which time is more nimble than memory, is the reason which induces me to keep a Journal.' She burned her first manuscript, *The History of Caroline Evelyn*. In 1777 she wrote, 'The fear of discovery, or of suspicion in the house, made copying extremely laborious to me.'

Burney's journal stayed constant, a proving ground for any emerging writer. Between 1768–86, it recorded her literary apprenticeship. The diary assumed multiple shapes and roles: a writer's working notebook, experiments in memoir, passages often composed as letters. The diary's rich complexity directly inspired her first novel, *Evelina*, written in the form of a letter. Published anonymously in 1778, it proved an instant success, followed in 1782 by another satiric novel, *Cecilia*. Their success won her a place as lady-in-waiting to Queen Charlotte. On 6 July 1786 she began a five-year stint in court. Initially, it provided fodder for her diary, ideal for Burney's pitch-perfect ear for the betraying idiosyncrasies of insincere speech.

Burney's diaries for 1786–91 show the double-razor edge of fame. Far worse than her father's critical voice was 'this dead and tame life'. Burney's diary reveals the deepest constriction for any writer: an inner or creative life not fed by the outer world. Endless days of court distraction caused exhaustion and anxiety. Forced to work in stolen time and away from prying eyes, she wrote in secrecy. Burney often made notations on erasable ivory tablets. Shorthand portraits made in pocket almanacs were later recreated fully as scenes and sent to her sister Susan as 'journal-diaries'. In October 1788 she began a play. On 19 October she notes, 'Had not this composition fit seized me, societyless, and bookless, and viewless as I am, I know not how I could have whiled away my being; but my tragedy goes on, and fills up all vacancies.'

After leaving court, Burney published *Camilla* and *The Wanderer*, her 1792–1839 diaries take on historic importance. Married now to a French exile, she witnessed the aftermath of the French Revolution and then Waterloo. Burney's conscious, hard-won internal freedom infused her voluminous letters. But the eight-volume diary remained her masterwork, offering a bracing, often cautionary look at creativity freeing itself of constriction. In 1843 Macaulay rued her career, 'too long at Court. She was sinking into a slavery worse than that of the body. The iron was beginning to enter the soul.'

Fanny Burney's writer's diary helped Virginia Woolf imagine her own. In 1919 Woolf noted, 'There looms ahead of me the shadow of some kind of form which a diary might attain to. I might in the course of time learn what it is that one can make

of this loose, drifting material of life; finding another use for it...
more consciously and scrupulously in fiction.' If Pepys' diary
is the gold standard for recording the loose drifting of daily
life, then Virginia Woolf's is the mother load of ore awaiting
transformation into creative work. From 1915 until her death in
1941, Woolf achieved the twentieth-century's most intimate portrait of a writer's working life – a time-lapse look at a diarist moving from aspiring writer in her mid-twenties to a published
novelist, noting, 'There's no doubt in my mind that I have found
out how to begin (at 40) to say something in my own voice... and
that interests me so that I feel I can go ahead without praise.'

Woolf's writer diaries find their true start in 1917, resumed
after a breakdown she suffered in 1915. The thirty notebooks filled
over the next twenty-seven years are indelibly shaped by that two-
year gap in diary keeping. Until the final diary entry on 24 March
1941, Woolf trains an unflinching eye on the fluctuations of the
creative psyche. The full diary, published as five volumes in 1977,
minutely records the doubt-plagued process that yielded nine
novels, a biography and six volumes of essays. What emerges is
a singular portrait of a writer's tenacity, both literary and personal. Invention and revision are the diary's hallmarks. It captures
a writer's epic struggle with reinvention on the page and within
herself. Between 1931 and 1941 Woolf achieved what no female
diarist had done, providing a detail-rich portrait of a writer at
midlife, minutely recording public success.

'I can trace some increase of ease in my professional writing
which I attribute to my casual half hours after tea.' By 1919, the
diary's specific method was established. For twenty-seven years,
reflecting on a morning's work, she scribbled at a 'rapid haphaz-
ard gallop'. The method silenced the inner critic and uncovered
'the diamonds of the dustheap'. While not kept daily, the diary
was a disciplined spur to ongoing work. 'In this book I practise
writing,' she observed. 'I shall invent my next book here.'

Woolf's diaries provide an exhaustive account of literary composition, the daily honing of craft drafting and revising. 'I write

variations of every sentence; compromises; bad shots; possibilities; till my writing book is like a lunatic's dream. Then I trust to some inspiration on rereading; & pencil them into some sense.' The diary records the intricate process of discovery and all that sabotaged it – work ruined by migraine or interruption. Woolf's diary reveals the balancing act between solitude and sociability. It allowed her to observe and discount moods, often distancing herself from depression, slipping back into the steady concentrated rhythms of work.

The diaries chart major breakthroughs in craft: finding her voice as a writer midway through *Jacob's Room* in 1921; discovering the 'tunneling process, by which I tell the past by installments' when writing *Mrs Dalloway* in 1924; transmuting the deep reach of memory of childhood summers in Cornwall and portraits of her parents in *To The Lighthouse* in 1926, and experimenting with style in *The Waves* in 1930. The diary often records her strategy of moving from fiction to essays whenever she was stuck.

Woolf's diaries proved invaluable during dry spells. 'I have spent the whole morning reading old diaries, & am now (10 to 1) much refreshed,' she wrote in 1932. A diarist's greatest resistance – rereading old entries – became a writer's tool. While writing *The Years*, she returned for details about pre-war London. Her 1931–5 diary covers the novel's four-year process – ten title changes, two years of nightmarish revision, cutting 700 down to 420 pages. 'It is worth mentioning for future reference, that the creative power which bubbles so pleasantly on beginning a new book quiets down after a time, & one goes on more steadily. Doubts creep in. Then one becomes resigned. Determination not to give in, & the sense of an impending shape keep one at it more than anything.'

Woolf's diary entry for 12 January 1923 records the death of Katherine Mansfield. Together their diaries offer a detailed portrait of literary friendship and rivalry. Between 1917–19, they often met weekly as 'a public of two', both writers using a diary to practise craft and plan stories or novels. In 1927 Woolf reviewed Mansfield's posthumously published *Journal*. At the height of her creative powers, Mansfield had noted, 'I am 33. Yet I am only just beginning to see now what it is I want to do. It will take years of work to really bring it off... How unbearable it would be to die – leave "scraps", "bits", nothing real finished.'

Katherine Mansfield's writer's diary shows creativity shaped by adversity. Between 1920–2 the journal records a race between the surge of her best stories and the tuberculosis she'd die of in 1923. 'Write about a doctor's waiting room,' she noted, 'the glass doors with the sun from outside shining through; the autumn trees pale and fine; the cyclamen, like wax.' In rented rooms in France, Italy and Switzerland, Mansfield mined her journals for material for the final short stories, including 'At the Bay'. Illness, envy, heartbreak – everything had its use. 'My sciatica!' she jotted. 'Remember to give to someone in a story.'

By 1922 the journal is filled with reading lists, story titles, character names. 'It's very strange, but the mere act of writing anything is a help. It seems to speed one on one's way.' 'Taking the Veil' is written in three hours. The journal's earliest preoccupations – financial and marital strains, literary in-fighting, posturing, compromises – give way to examining consciousness itself. In adversity, the working journal becomes a creative companion but also a way 'to lose all that is superficial and acquired in me and to become a conscious, direct human being'.

Sylvia Plath's diaries ended with her suicide in London on 11 February 1963. The final diary recording the seven months when she produced her breakthrough *Ariel* poems had been thought lost or destroyed. Hailed as 'a genuine literary event' when published in 2000, *The Journals of Sylvia Plath 1950–1962* are a 674-page portrait of disciplined ambition. From college to her graduate years at Cambridge, Plath used the diary to test her talent and quicken her resolve. Between 1956–62, after her marriage to poet Ted Hughes, Plath's diary assumes another ambition: the challenge of literary equals.

1958: the year I stop teaching and start writing. Ted's faith: don't expect: just write: what? It will take months to get my inner world peopled, and the people moving. How else to do it but plunge out of this safe scheduled time-clock wage-check world into my own voids. Distant planets spin: I dream too much of fame, posturings, a novel into print. But with no job, no money worries, why, the black lid should lift. Look at life with humor: easy to say, things open up: know people: horizons extend.

The twenty-three original journals, including two Ted Hughes unsealed before his death in 1998, show Plath constantly extending literary horizons – trying out styles, tabulating acceptance rates, eyeing her competition on both sides of the Atlantic, finding new markets for the poems. 'It is as if my life were magically run by two electric currents: joyous positive and despairing negative,' she records. The 'black lid' in her 1958 entry signals poetry written despite battling both depression and crippling perfectionism. The journals detail the bracing necessity of routine. Cooking, cycling, walking, gardening, reading fill the journal's index. Anxious about the writing tasks she'd set for herself, she wrote, 'Will it come and will we do it? Answer me, book.'

The posthumous publication of writers' diaries is a unique footnote in the history of diaries. Woolf's and Mansfield's posthumous diaries became a small industry and steady revenue stream for the husbands. Mansfield's husband, critic Middleton Murray, assembled the whirlwind of Mansfield's notebooks, ledgers, exercise books and published them as one journal in 1927. A first royalty cheque netted him in a year ten times what she had made in a short lifetime. Leonard Woolf continued to help his wife's career even after her death. In 1917 he'd set up the Hogarth Press so she could write freely without worrying about publication judgement. In 1953 he published *A Writer's Diary*, an abridged version that selected excerpts from the diary that 'discusses the day-to-day problems of plot or form, of character or exposition, which she encounters in each of her books as she conceived them or writes or revises them'.

Diaries in service of another's creativity hold their own category. In 1798 twenty-six-year-old Dorothy Wordsworth started a journal 'because I shall give Wm. pleasure by it.' Her 1798 notebooks and 1800–03 journal were an open contract to record and aid her brother's creativity. 'She gave me eyes,' he noted. Her *Grasmere Journal* also gave him poems. 'The Beggar' originated from an entry Dorothy had made two years earlier when he was away. An April 1802 entry recording a walk taken together to Gowbarrow Park inspired his famous poem 'I Wandered Lonely as a Cloud'.

Her journal is often read for clues to her brother's creative life, as well as for portraits of Coleridge and other Lake District poets. Dorothy possessed the eye of a naturalist and the instinct of a poet. Her *Grasmere Journal* contains some of the finest nature writing any diarist has produced, 'As I lay down on the grass I observed the glittering silver line on the ridge of the backs of the sheep, owing to their situation respecting the sun, which made them look beautiful, but with something of strangeness, like animals of another kind, as if belonging to a more splendid world.' The diarist, who had noted in 1810 'I should detest the idea of setting myself up as an Author', might be shocked to know her journals have never been out of print.

The curious case of diarist Alice James, sister of novelist Henry and philosopher William, shows the more complicated task for a diarist within a creative family. Overwhelmed by family pressure, Alice chose two ways to distinguish herself: illness and a diary. Settling in England in 1884, she lived near her novelist brother. In 1889 she abandoned her commonplace book of others' quotations and started a diary. The witty and acerbic diary examined the price of bottled-up talent. After Alice's death in 1892, her famous brothers saw why they had once likened her to 'bottled lightning'. Unaware she'd been recording them, Henry called the diary 'heroic in its individuality... Her style, her power to write – are indeed to me a delight.' He then burned the diary. Fortunately, her companion had three copies printed privately.

Caroline Fox's 1835–71 diary is crammed with portraits of observed literary life. 'Carlyle wandered down to tea looking dusky and aggrieved at having to live in such a generation,' she notes, later recording that Wordsworth 'evidently loves the monologue style of conversation... his general appearance that of the abstract thinker'.

Surely the most famous diarists providing an eye on literary life, though, are the Goncourt brothers. Artists turned novelists, they kept a shared journal between 1851 and 1870. After Jules's death in 1870, Edmond continued the journal until 1896. Writers from Balzac to Baudelaire appear in it, as do artists from Degas to Rodin. The Goncourt brothers wrote six novels together and their journals offer invaluable information about creative process.

> Flaubert said to us today: 'The story, plot of a novel is of no interest to me. When I write a novel I aim at rendering a colour, a shade... In Madame Bovary, all I wanted to do was to render a grey colour, the mouldy colour of a wood-louse's experience. The story of the novel mattered so little to me that a few days before starting on it I still had in mind a very different Madame Bovary from the one I created: the setting and the overall tone were the same, but she was to have been a chaste and devout old maid. And then I realised that she would have been an impossible character.'

Twentieth-century writers' diaries expose the cautionary under-side of creative life – gin-soaked nights and blank creative mornings in F. Scott Fitzgerald's or John Cheever's journals. Anxiety-paralysing afternoons in Kafka's and Plath's. Camus rues, 'I spent all my time thinking about K. Mansfield, about that long, painful and tender struggle against illness.' From 1935–60, his literary notebooks stockpiled working titles, dialogue and story ideas. 'I sometimes need to write things which I cannot completely control but which therefore prove that what is in me is stronger than I am.' Camus fortified himself by setting epic goals, often as numbered lists. For the summer of June 1938,

1) Finish Florence and Algiers
2) Caligula
3) The summer impromptu
4) Essay on the theatre
5) Essay on the forty-hour week
6) Rewrite novel.

Kafka's diaries show the torment of a young writer still living at home. 'I want to write, with a constant trembling on my forehead. I sit in my room in the very headquarters of the uproar of the entire house. I hear all the doors close... I hear even the slamming of the oven door in the kitchen. My father bursts through the doors of my room and passes through in his dragging dressing gown.' Two years later, he captures that claustrophobic horror before meeting future in-laws. The 1913 entry foreshadows his famous story 'Metamorphosis' of 1915, when the narrator wakes to discover he's been turned into a dung beetle. He records, 'agonies in bed toward morning. Saw only solution in jumping out of the window. My mother came to my bedside and asked whether I had sent off the letter and whether it was my original text. I said it was the original text, but made even sharper.'

In Kafka's writer diaries, alienation is the hallmark of twentieth-century life. Public exposure and private humiliation hound the already famous Evelyn Waugh. In his diary for 25 August 1947 he writes of arriving in Oslo, 'The town airless and dusty in unusual heat, the inhabitants straggling about the streets in their shirt-sleeves eating ice-cream. The Grand Hotel in the builders' hands; constant hammering... A midget female socialist came to introduce herself as my agent and took me to see my publisher, who hasn't published anything yet.'

'In how one lives as a private person is intimately bound into the work,' poet and novelist May Sarton noted in her diary. Her 1968 memoir, *Plant Dreaming Deep*, had chronicled her move to a small New Hampshire town as a single woman after a lifetime in literary circles. Nearing sixty, Sarton began a journal covering the same period but reflecting on everything the memoir had omitted – the lonely underside of creative life. *Journal of a Solitude*, published in 1973, became an international bestseller. From 1973–96, Sarton published seven journals, each devoted to a single year. The journals record a late-life creative sprint, from sixty to eighty-two, as she sustained her work despite the inevitable hardships of ageing.

'Every grief or inexplicable seizure by weather, woe, or work can – if we discipline ourselves and think hard enough – be turned to account,' she noted. In 1980 she published *Recovering: a Journal*, resuming writing after breast cancer. *After the Stroke* chronicled the slow return to poetry in 1988. Her late journals, *Endgame: A Journal of the Seventy-Ninth Year* and *At Eighty-Two*, show a writer's self-imposed routine and discipline: rising at six-thirty; juggling the poetry and the now-famous journals, worrying if advances would cover the heating bill. Incapacitated by illness at eighty-two, Sarton dictated her final journal into a tape recorder.

I always forget how important the empty days are, how important it may be sometimes not to expect to produce anything, even a few lines in a journal. I am still pursued by a neurosis about work inherited from my father. A day where one has not pushed oneself to the limit seems a damaged damaging day, a sinful day. Not so! The most valuable thing we can do for the psyche, occasionally, is to let it rest, wander, live in the changing light of a room.

Woolf read Fanny Burney's diaries; Plath read Woolf's; Sarton read about herself in volume five of Woolf's diary. Writers have also long turned to other creative diaries for inspiration. Composer Benjamin Britten's *The Journeying Boy: Diaries 1928–38* chart his early musical apprenticeship, preparing him for his operatic masterpiece *Peter Grimes* and later collaborations with Auden, Isherwood and MacNeice. Modern choreographer Martha Graham destroyed her early journals and letters, but saved fifty notebooks from the 1940s to mid-1960s. *The Notebooks of Martha Graham* reveal the 'inner landscape' of creative ideas behind her master dance works, *Errand into the Maze*, *Clytemnestra* and *Deaths and Entrances*.

Even if no artist comes close to possessing the creative genius displayed in da Vinci's 5,000-page notebooks, many artists have left notebooks and journals. In Benjamin Robert Haydon's twenty-seven-volume 1808–46 journals, the cash-strapped artist notes the perfect timing of selling a painting. 'Now, Reader, who-ever thou art – young & thoughtless, or old and reflecting,' he writes on 21 April 1843. 'Today – this very day – I have sold my Curtius, when only yesterday I had no hope, & my heart beat, & my head whirled, & my hand shook at my distress, I had taken the butter knife off the Table to raise 13/-.'

In his *Intimate Journals* Paul Gauguin broods about his Post-Impressionist life and chosen exile in Tahiti. Offering frank assess-ments of Van Gogh, Cézanne, Manet and Monet, he examines his own envy of Degas. An entry in *The Notebooks of Edgar Degas* would have soothed Gauguin. 'It seems to me today that if one seriously wants to create art and make a little original corner for oneself; or at least keep for oneself the most innocent of person-alities, it is necessary to strengthen oneself in solitude.' In thirty-eight notebooks, Degas made over 1,300 drawings amid reflections about distraction and peer pressure, 'there is too much talk and gossip; pictures are apparently made, like stock-market prices'.

In 1832 painter Eugene Delacroix travelled to Morocco to refresh his imagination. Along with his sketchbook he also

brought his journal, a habit begun at twenty-three that continued for nearly forty years until his death in 1863. His Morocco
stay lasted only six months, but it transformed his sense of
colour and improvisational work methods. Often jotting notes
next to quick pencil and watercolour sketches, Delacroix began
one of the most illuminating records of any working artist. That
motivation was already present in his first entry, 'I am carrying
out my plan, so often formulated, of keeping a journal. What
I most keenly wish is not to forget that I am writing for myself
alone. Thus I shall always tell the truth.' Whenever he was weary
or uninspired, he only needed to reread his own advice, 'What
moves men of genius, or rather, what inspires their work, is
not new ideas, but their obsession with the idea that what has
already been said is still not enough.'

Nineteenth – Twentieth Century: War Diaries

When the war ends I'll be at the crossroads; and I know the path to choose. I must go out into the night alone.

– Siegfried Sassoon, Diary, 1916

The most famous war diary first nestled among nine other birthday gifts. A red plaid cloth journal amid books and sweets. To mark the day, 12 June 1942, the diarist wrote, 'I hope I will be able to confide everything to you, as I have never been able to confide in anyone, and I hope you will be a great source of comfort and support.' In the next day's entry, 'Writing in a diary is really a strange experience for someone like me. Not only because I've never written anything before, but also because it seems to me that later on neither I nor anyone else will be interested in the musings of a thirteen-year-old school girl.'

The diarist, of course, is Anne Frank. She is writing what's destined to become the most widely read diary in history. And it is history that she's concerned with – her own and the world outside that she'll soon only be able to glimpse at night. In the diary's fourth entry she's already aware of the Secret Annex being prepared for her family. Before 6 July 1942, when her family is forced into hiding, Frank uses the diary to trace this wartime fate – her own birth in 1929; emigrating from Frankfurt to Amsterdam in 1933; the 1938 pogroms; the Nazi invasion of the Netherlands in May 1940; the entrenched occupation that interrupts her schooling and her father's work. In her final weeks of freedom, she rues the ever-increasing restrictions on Jews – forced to wear yellow stars, forbidden to sit in their own gardens, banned from taking public transport.

War, isolation, Holocaust – these are the realities that drove Frank and seven family and friends into hiding between 1942 and 1944. They are also the conditions under which Frank wrote that indelibly shaped her as a diarist. The Secret Annex, a vacant attic space in Otto Frank's three-storey office building, was accessible only by a staircase concealed by a bookcase. In 1944 when the family was arrested, fifteen-year-old Frank travelled one last time down that staircase, unaware she had left history its most famous diary. A war diary kept not by a soldier but by a diarist who embodied everything that war fought to preserve: the ordinariness of daily life – a child doing her homework, making reading lists, dreaming of movie stars whose photos she tacks on the bedroom wall. Until 4 August 1944, when Nazis spilled her diary's loose pages on the floor, the claustrophobic Annex was 'a little piece of blue heaven surrounded by black, black rain clouds'. Frank records air raids overhead, fighting outside, news on the radio that seals her diary's destiny.

During World War II, Allied forces discouraged diary keeping as it posed security risks. As if mirroring that fear, Frank deposited her diary nightly in her father's briefcase. Only in 1945, as a survivor, did Otto Frank read the diary of his daughter who had perished at Bergen-Belsen. Ever since its first 1947 publication, tens of millions of readers have discovered what Otto Frank first saw in Anne's diary: a child maturing into an adult before one's eyes, fighting loneliness and anxiety. But it also showed a diary's capacity to shelter and transform a self in extremity. Anne Frank's diary provides the clearest link between war, trauma and creativity. It sets the standard against which all war diaries, past and present, are measured.

Frank's war diary is a psychological *tour de force*, but also a frame-by-frame glimpse of a literary apprenticeship. From the moment she turns a birthday autograph book into a diary, invention and discipline are its hallmarks. By the fifth entry, 20 June 1942, Anne addresses an ideal imagined reader, 'Dearest Kitty'. The diary is composed as a series of letters, giving its entries their intimacy and spontaneity. It allows her to experiment with perspective, often writing about herself in the third person. 'I have one outstanding trait in my character, which must strike anyone who knows me for any length of time, and that is my self-knowledge. I can watch myself and my actions, just like an outsider.'

War had already turned her inward; life in the Secret Annex forced her into deeper observation of invented normalcy – two families setting up steady routines; parents instilling discipline and rules. The diary's continuity is a daily psychological victory over war's discontinuity. By late 1942, Anne had filled the original diary. From 12 June 1942 to 5 December 1943, she wrote in a cloth diary, then in a series of three exercise books. On 22 January 1944 she reread the entire diary. It had become partly a 'book of memoirs', recording life under intensifying Nazi assault. Like the radio or the Annex's secret helpers bringing in news, her diary remained the link to the outside world. Normally, war diaries are the intersection of the private in the public sphere. Frank's is the opposite, written in isolation but aware of millions on the outside trapped by bombing and destruction. As the family listened to the radio, the same news was being heard by BBC listeners in London during the Blitz. Frank's hopes and fears correspond directly to the pushpins on a map kept near the radio that tracked Allied movements.

On 29 March 1944 Frank heard a radio broadcast from London. Gerrit Bolkestein, a member of the Dutch government in exile, wanted to publish first-hand accounts of the war. She records her wish to become a journalist, 'whether I shall succeed or not, I cannot say, but my diary will be a great help'. Frank now assumed the role of diarist witness. All subsequent entries underscore the psychological resilience necessary to sustain it.

On 11 May 1944 she writes of hoping to publish a book after the war entitled *The Secret Annex*. While continuing her ongoing diary, she began revising her earlier writing. Anne began editing the diary in the late spring and early summer of 1944.

War, she noted, is 'a contradiction imposed from without and one imposed within'. The diary's revisions chart not only her own growth as a writer, but Frank's larger awareness of her responsibility – and credibility – as a witness. How she revised her diary is inextricably linked to how war had deeply clarified perspective. The diary's style shifts to the direct testimony of a witness. No longer a diarist writing to herself, she's a writer carefully recording for others – for posterity. Increasingly aware of her role as a narrator, she revised sections, deleted passages, adding others, working from memory. The diary's multiple shifting perspectives allowed her to see old hurts in a new light – her mother preferring Margot, the better-behaved older sister, or her father's unhappiness over her infatuation with Peter van Pels. As a protective cloak, she invented pseudonyms for the Annex's inhabitants and helpers.

By the time of her arrest, Anne had rewritten nearly two-thirds of her diary. She had revised up to 29 March 1944, copying it on to loose sheets. One entry she kept unchanged. It mused on the game the Secret Annex residents played, imagining what they would first do if and when they were free. On 1 August 1944, the last sentence Anne Frank wrote in her diary was, 'I keep trying to find a way to become what I'd like to be and what I could be if... if only there were no other people in the world.'

The diary was first mentioned in a Dutch newspaper story on 3 April 1946, citing its pages were as moving as 'all the evidence of Nuremberg put together'. Working with Anne's original version A and her revised B, Otto Frank submitted the diary for publication under the title Anne had imagined – *Het Achterhuis* (*The Annexe*). First published in the Netherlands in 1947, it appeared in Germany and France in 1950; in Britain and America in 1952, retitled *The Diary of a Young Girl*, its preface written by Eleanor

Roosevelt. The diary's immortality was immediate: a single voice that stood for the six million silenced. But it also formulated the question every war diary poses: *If things had gone differently in life. If everyone had survived.* In 1997 the full unabridged diary appeared. Otto Frank had omitted some entries out of respect for the family that had perished. The 1995 edition also restored several entries that showed the still idealistic Anne often far more critical of the horrors of war.

Four miles from the Secret Annex, at 6 Gabriel Metsustraat, twenty-seven-year-old diarist Etty Hillesum documented the war in eight exercise books. Her entries recorded war as a civilian activist. On 27 July 1942 she notes finding an envelope in the morning's post. 'I was quite calm and thought, "My call-up notice"', the same official summons that had sent the Franks into hiding. Hillesum, a law graduate, intellectual and social activist, opted to live and work openly, knowing that it placed her at maximum risk. Hillesum's diary, published to international acclaim in 1983 as *An Interrupted Life*, provides one of the most acutely observed portraits of a diarist transformed by war. It offers a unique view of Hillesum's dual response to war: her volunteer work within Jewish transit refugee camps and her intensified psychological need to serve others. Paradoxically, Hillesum's 1941–3 war diary, now a twentieth-century classic, is one of inner liberation, a complex spiritual autobiography, later hailed as 'a testimony of faith, hope and love – written in hell'.

'I want to be there at every front,' Hillesum wrote towards the end of her diary. 'I don't ever want to be what they call "safe".' Closer to its start, she reread two diary entries. 10 November 1941: 'Mortal fear in every fibre. Complete collapse. Lack of self confidence. Aversion. Panic.' 3 July 1942: 'Very well then, this new certainty.' That second entry acknowledges that unless liberated by Allied troops, her own death was certain. Until then, she wouldn't 'burden others' with her fears. She resolved to live and work 'with the same conviction', making others' lives, not would just her own, as safe as possible. The diary she'd keep for the final two years of her life examined just that. Until her death at twenty-nine, Hillesum records a war-rav- aged world seemingly deserted by God that she was slowly start- ing to find.

On 15 July 1942 Hillesum records taking a position with the Jewish Council. Two weeks later, she notes success – her requested reassignment to Westerbork, the refugee camp, work- ing for the department of 'Social Welfare for People in Transit'. The same transit camp where she would soon be one of 101,000 Dutch Jews transported to Auschwitz. Hillesum started her volunteer work three days after Anne Frank had begun her diary. The two diaries are often read in sequence. It's tempting to see Hillesum's diary as a continuation, an adult psychologically and creatively coming of age in impossible circumstances. The diary Hillesum starts on 9 March 1941 also chronicles a literary ambi- tion. Yet war profoundly recasts Hillesum's ambition. From 1941–3, the diary shows the shift from a desire to write, to being loved, to knowing God.

Hillesum's diary testifies to a timeless search for meaning while objectively recording all that threatens to extinguish it. 'All that words should do is lend silence form,' she observed of a diarist's role in documenting war and inner life. Hillesum's literary eye and psychological acuity – sharpened by her mentor, Julius Spier – shape her first-person accounts. On 28 July 1942 she records a Wednesday morning spent in a crowded Gestapo hall as she and others have their fate debated. The diary's lens includes both oppressor and oppressed. 'All of us occupied the same space, the men behind the desk no less than those about to be questioned. What distinguished each one of us was only our inner attitudes.' As a Gestapo official mocks, 'I thought him more pitiable than those he shouted at, and those he shouted at I thought pitiable for being afraid of him. When it was my turn to stand in front of him, he bawled at me, "What the hell's so funny?" I wanted to say, "Nothing's funny here except you."' Hillesum's spiritual discipline lends the diary its power of distancing. 'You cannot know another's inner life from his circumstances,' she notes. Character is a choice to 'determine his inner responses'.

On 5 July 1943, she records losing her travel status. The diary's late entries from Westerbork echo many of Anne Frank's. Despite suffering and injustice, she refuses to be consumed by hatred. 'All the appalling things that happen are no mysterious threats from afar, but arise from fellow beings very close to us. That makes these happenings more familiar, then, and not so frightening.' The final third of the journal is composed of letters from Westerbork. Red Cross workers later found the last one she'd thrown from the narrow cattle car window. It survives, as does her earlier notation, 'Every day I shall put my papers in order and every day I shall say farewell. And the real farewell, when it comes, will only be a small outward confirmation of what has been accomplished within me from day to day.'

Viktor Klemperer, a journalist and professor, survived the war. His 1933–45 diaries were first published in 1998 in two volumes, *I Shall Bear Witness* and *To the Bitter End*. Though a Protestant convert married to a Christian, he was still subject to arrest. The diaries are a minutely observed look at the human pathology of war. As a diarist, Klemperer captures the claustrophobic horror in small details – the milkmaid not allowed to deliver to Jewish homes; toothpaste tubes stamped with a swastika; three doorbell rings as just one is the Gestapo. Klemperer's diary is noteworthy for its steady account of the way in which Nazi propaganda distorted the German language. Its pages track euphemisms – 'special treatment' for murder; 'pick up' for arrest; 'evacuation' for deportation. His diaries provided invaluable material for his book, *LTI – Lingua Tertii Imperii*, that examined the doublespeak of fascism and tyranny.

World War II diarists inherited the moral eloquence of the previous generation's war diarists. World War I produced a unique hybrid: the poet soldier diarist. Siegfried Sassoon, along with fellow soldiers, Wilfred Owen and Robert Graves, served in some of the bloodiest trench warfare on the Western Front. Sassoon embodies the diarist's conflicting need to record and transcend what's been witnessed. What came to be known as the poetry of shellshock was first registered in diaries and letters like his. Sassoon's 1915–18 diaries contain important portraits of Graves and Owen, documenting collective creativity born of trauma. His wartime diaries provided the raw inspiration for poems such as 'Words for the Wordless', immortalising the seventeen million dead. 'Again the dead, the dead again demanding/ To be, O not to be remembered strongly.'

Sassoon enlisted, serving as a cavalry trooper a day after war had been declared. Between 1914–19, he saw some of the heaviest fighting on the Western Front, and later was awarded the Military Cross, which he threw into the Mersey River in 1917. His 1915–18 diaries chart the slow moral outrage of a soldier moving from a rural, fox-hunting childhood to World War I's blood-soaked soil and muddy trench warfare. Toughened and traumatised, Sassoon used his diary so that even once bucolic poems took on a creative maturity and urgency. In September 1915, his first war poem, 'Absolution', signalled the theme which was to become the preoccupation of his war diary – the 'loss of things desired'. Just as the war poems resulted directly from Sassoon's combat, his diary served as a repository for his celebrated post-war trilogy, which relied heavily on his earlier diaries.

Constant threat of danger and interminable waiting in trenches sharpened Sassoon's power of observation as a diarist. In a 1916 entry, he evokes the whizzing menace of battle, infusing it with poetry,

As I sit in the sun in a nook among the sandbags and chalky debris, with shells flying overhead in the blue air, a lark sings... Shells rend and bury, and vibrate and scatter, hurling fragments and lumps and jagged splinters at you; they lift you off your legs and leave you huddled and bleeding and torn and scorched... Heaven is furious with the smoke and flare and portent of shells, but bullets are a swarm of whizzing hornets, mad, winged and relentless… There are still pools in the craters; they reflect the stars like any lovely water, but nothing grows near them.

Sassoon's diaries slowly chart his inner life becoming 'far more real' than 'this land of the warzone'. In 1915 he noted, 'The last fifteen months have unsealed my eyes.' Like countless soldiers, he recognises that he's unable to return to the old life. 'I want freedom, not comfort', he noted in his diary. By 1917, images of the dead piled in trenches and gnawed by rats made their way into poems like 'Dreaming'. Both Graves and Sassoon had fought in the Battle of the Somme where 623,000 troops perished. British casualties numbered 60,000 on the battle's first day. Sassoon's diary's for 1 July 1918 records a soldier lying on his side, his arms still moving, 'his head was a crimson patch'.

Such details stored in his diary were indelibly seared in Sassoon's psyche. His April–June 1917 diary records three events that changed his life and the fate of war poetry. Unwilling to support the war, he signed a protest letter. In his diary he wrote, 'On behalf of those who are suffering now, I make this protest against the deception which is being practised on them.' Graves, who had served alongside Sassoon in the Royal Welsh Fusiliers, convinced military officials that Sassoon was suffering from shellshock. Sassoon's diary recounts his treatment at Craiglockhart Hospital in Edinburgh, where he met fellow soldier and poet, Wilfred Owen. Sassoon introduced him to Graves, whom Sassoon had first met in November 1915 when Graves was in A Company of the 1st Battalion. While Owen was killed shortly after returning to the front in 1918, the three soldier poets had galvanised each other's creative talent. Owen's posthumous fame owes much to his fellow soldiers, especially Sassoon who was the first to edit a volume of Owen's poetry, extensively annotating Owen's 'Anthem for a Doomed Youth'.

Sassoon's diary entries over five months at Craiglockhart record him writing his best war poems. He often pasted letters into his diary, the public and private playing off the other – participant soldier, observer diarist. Throughout April 1917, he records soldiers playing cards on the table opposite his bed; remembering blood spreading across soldiers' pale faces like 'ink spilt on blotting paper'. He rues, 'the kindly immunity of the hospital is what they longed for when they shivered and waited for the attack to begin, or the brutal bombardment to cease'. On 15 June 1917 he noted that he wrote for 'those who are suffering now'.

Between 1931 and 1932 Sassoon copied out passages from his 1923–25 diaries and destroyed the originals. Sassoon's diaries provided the raw material for his three award-winning fictionalised autobiographies, the satiric *Memoirs of a Fox-Hunting Man* (1928), and the searing *Memoirs of an Infantry Officer* (1930) and *Sherston's Progress* (1936). But it's the war poetry, material first recorded in his diaries and then transformed into poems written in the trenches, that is Sassoon's real legacy. It places him in the creative company of John Masefield, later Poet Laureate, who fought at Gallipoli; and poet Edmund Blunden who later wrote *Undertones of War*. On 11 November 1985, a slate stone was erected in Westminster Abbey's Poet's Corner to commemorate sixteen Great War poets, among them Sassoon, Owen and Graves. The inscription is from Owen, 'My subject is War, and the pity in War./The Poetry is in the pity.'

'Saturday: Up late (about 6 A.M.) and went out to the castle. Photographed the castle at S.E. angle: where the moat turns and above which is one of the very few crusader walls in existence here. It is patched in front (to R.) with Arab wall, but is very fine. A wide-angle photo.' The diarist is T.E. Lawrence. The twenty-two-year-old was in northern Syria in 1911 as a field archaeologist. He was observing fortifications built by Crusaders, travelling on foot to other archaeological sites to study fortification design. The area's sites and the opportunity to map the area's sites was desired by both British and German intelligence.

The previous year the Germans had started constructing the Baghdad railway through northern Syria. Future German troops would be able to bypass the British-run Suez Canal. By 1916 he was Lieutenant Colonel Lawrence, a liaison officer and in the unique position of being able to provide first-hand information of the area, the kind detailed in his 1911 diary. During the 1916–18 Arab Revolt, Lawrence was its most famous Western participant. He kept notebooks and was a prolific letter writer, including to friend, poet and soldier Robert Graves. In 1919, while changing trains in Reading, Lawrence lost the manuscript of *Seven Pillars of Wisdom*, his memoir recounting his Arab Revolt years. He had destroyed his wartime notes and later was forced to write from memory. Poet soldier Robert Graves later became Lawrence's biographer. From his own memoir, *Goodbye to All That* and *The Long Weekend, 1918–39*, he knew that post-war books owed everything to earlier notes or diaries.

'God forgive us but ours is a *monstrous* system and wrong and iniquity.' The sentence is underlined in another diarist's first pages. This diary's entry wasn't made by one of the thousands of soldiers scribbling in trenches, but by a diarist who often had daily access to war generals. The 18 March 1861 entry commentating on slavery was written one month before the start of the American Civil War, 1861–5, when eleven southern slave-owning states seceded and formed the Confederate States of America. The tragedy of a nation at war with itself was captured in thousands of surviving diaries. But none is more epic or powerful than Mary Chestnut's.

Chestnut's 800 page diary is a vast social canvas – of auctioned slaves, misguided generals, lowly soldiers and the elite architects of a doomed war that left one million dead and four million slaves freed. The diary's originality lies in its perspective – Chestnut is an insider who writes with the perspective of an outsider. As a diarist she was in a unique position, recording Lincoln's Washington and the Confederate South to which her

United States Senator husband returned. Witnessing war in four southern states, she dined often with Confederate Generals Robert E. Lee and Jefferson Davis, who were both unaware of her anguish over slavery. When the full diary was published in 1982, it won the Pulitzer Prize. 'What Samuel Pepys' diary was to the reign of Charles II,' one reviewer wrote, 'Mary Chestnut's is to the Confederacy.'

At the start of the war, Chestnut's diary was a red leather-bound journal; by the end, she's writing on the back pages of an old recipe book. The handwriting is often rushed, entries secretly created while Generals Robert E. Lee and Jefferson Davis were nearby. In Chestnut's hands, the diary creates a parallel drama: the consequences of war played out in a nation divided, brother against brother, but also within families on both sides, her own included. Born into a slave-owning family, Chestnut was a serious, voracious reader, fluent in French and German, an intellectual with literary ambitions. A fixture in southern salons, she had little patience for provincialism or its 'air of a watering place where one does not pay and where there are no strangers'. Yet the salons placed her in a unique position: being able to over-hear planning strategy that would end the world into which she was born.

Chestnut's diary shows the daily effects of war on both sides. She is among the first to visit and tend the sick and dying, noting the high amputation rates. On 20 September 1863 she writes of open railroad cars carrying sleeping Confederate soldiers. 'It was a strange sight – miles *apparently*, of platform cars – soldiers rolled in their blankets, lying in rows, heads all covered, fast asleep. In their gray blankets, packed in regular order, they looked like swathed mummies.' One soldier had a diary propped on his knee.

Keeping a war diary had given Chestnut not just a purpose, but a way to channel her considerable intelligence. 'My subjec-tive days are over,' she wrote in 1861, 'no more *silent* eating into my own heart.' Instead, the diary shows a nation eating into its own. Its lens is slavery's effect on all classes. The diary's most haunting entries involve slave women forced to have children by their owners. She's sickened by slave auctions. An 1863 entry details the raised platform block so the crowd can best see a slave who's been dressed in silks and satin to make her more saleable.

As the bitter legacy of slavery divides families, Chestnut the diarist sees what others are missing in front of their eyes. She evokes this in an 1863 entry written as a mini scene. Her father's slave butler Dick stands at a sideboard as his owners engage in an animated discussion at the table. Should slaves be allowed to join the depleted Confederate army? Dick listens as his owners wager which side slaves would join – theirs or the enemy's. Chestnut sits silently, storing the details for the diary. As a child, she had taught Dick how to read. She rues, 'He won't look at me now. He looks over my head – he scents freedom in the air.' He stands at the sideboard, waiting out the war, 'a very respectful Egyptian sphinx, so inscrutably silent is he'. Both he and Chestnut know the fortunes of those at the table were about to change forever.

Chestnut's diary unsentimentally records her own post-war reversals – finding pine cones for kindling, being unable to find a coin to pay a ferry fee. Mary Chestnut was fifty-eight, running an egg and dairy farm, when she reread her journals, making notes as she went. Like so many war diarists after her, she went back to the original and began revising entries. Between 1881 and 1884 she revised her wartime diary, redrafting close to 2,000 pages. 'I have always kept a journal after a fashion of my own, with dates... and I have kept letters and extracts from the papers.' Notations from 1861–4 were then fleshed out, many soon becoming fully realised scenes. In the two-decade interval, she'd drafted three novels. Her diary succeeded where the novels had failed.

To let the war and its stories emerge, she adopted a new diary strategy. Her new rule: 'leaving myself out'. Instead, she concentrated on selecting details that showed the arc of war. Among the diary's many notable scenes is the June 1861 entry in which

Chestnut awakens as her deaf sister-in-law Sally Chestnut is shouting outside, terrified by smelling smoke. In a frenzy, 'sixty or seventy people kept here to wait upon this household' try to calm a woman unaware of the larger war. As thousands of soldiers burn in battle, Chestnut records slaves catering to a woman afraid of fire. 'Candles have to be taken out of the room to be snuffed. Lamps are extinguished only in the porticoes – or further afield. She finds violets oppressive.' Chestnut rues, 'the bombardment of Fort Sumter was nothing to this'.

Chestnut's diary contains an extensive record of slave vernacular and colloquial speech. In the original diary a maid's presence is noted; in the revision, she's given her name, Molly, and quoted, scolding Chestnut for forgetting to lock away her diary. Often the power of what's *not* said lends scenes their inherent drama. For the October 1861 murder of Mrs Witherspoon by her own slaves, Chestnut lets details tell the story – a bloody handprint on a candlestick; the blanket's underside with 'again, bloody fingers'. Or of another slave owner hung by her neck from an apple tree to look like suicide. She was supposed to have walked to the tree, but her brand new shoes had never been worn, their soles never having touched the ground.

The interval war diaries wait to surface depends on history's judgement of the war that's recorded. Some diaries, like Frank's, are published almost immediately. Chestnut's diary remained unpublished until 1905, with only a fraction of it appearing nineteen years after her death. A second highly abridged version, *A Diary From Dixie*, appeared in 1949. Chestnut's forty-eight copybooks, 25,000 pages revised from the original diary, waited until historian C. Vann Woodward restored and annotated them. Published as *Mary Chestnut's Civil War*, it won the Pulitzer Prize.

Centuries of war diaries – from Sir Richard Grenville's 1625 and 1627 military diaries as naval commander, to Robert Douglas' 1644 Civil War diary and Thomas Bellingham's 1688–90 military diaries – are largely of historic interest. If war produces soldier writers, many of its best diaries are kept by writers observing war at close range. Simone de Beauvoir's *Wartime Diary 1939–41* chronicled life in occupied France. Arguably the finest writer's war diary seen through civilian eyes is Iris Origo's *War in the Val d'Orcia*. Between 1943 and 1944 Origo used her Tuscany home La Foce to shelter partisans and refugee children. She hid escaped Allied prisoners of war and helped a deserter with documents. While giving birth to a second daughter, she heard the groans of an airman whose leg had just been amputated. A 12 March 1944 entry describes listening to a broadcast given by a Pope unable to console 'the starving refugees who have flocked into the city'. Origo hears the sound of those gathered in the square, 'from thousands of throats came a cry of supplication, unforgettable by anyone who heard it – a cry which sounded like an echo of all the suffering that is torturing the world: "Give us peace; oh, give us peace."'

Twentieth – Twenty-First Century: Cyberspace and the Digital Diary

We do not wish to know how his imaginary hero, but how he, the actual hero, lived day to day.

– David Henry Thoreau, Journal, 21 October 1857

I had a lot of dates but I decided to stay home and dye my eyebrows.

– Andy Warhol, Diary, 11 March 1978

January – Etymology
Re-Latinised from Middle English *Ieneuer* < Old Norman French *genever* < Latin *inurius* ('(month) of Janus'), perhaps from Proto-Indo-European base **ei-*, 'to go'.

– Wiktionary

It takes 1.1 seconds to discover that January owes its word origin to Janus, the Roman god of doorways. Click another Wiki site and up pops a sculpted image of the god of auspicious beginnings and endings. Janus is shown in double profile, each face pointing in an opposite direction to suggest his gift of seeing past and future simultaneously. January has long been the starting point for the New Year, where, like Janus, diarists pause to look backwards and forward.

It's fitting then that in the centre of ancient Rome, the Vatican chose January to launch a new decree. On 23 January 2010 Pope

Benedict XVI urged priests: Go forth and blog. 'The spread of multimedia communications and its rich "menu of options" might make us think it sufficient simply to be present on the Web.' The Vatican challenged priests, 'to proclaim the Gospel by employing the latest generation of audiovisual resources (images, videos, animated features, blogs, Websites) which, alongside traditional means, can open up broad new vistas for dialogue'.

Yet the Vatican cautioned that, while interacting with the faithful on Facebook or Twitter, priests 'in the world of digital communication should be less notable for their media savvy than for their priestly heart'. The Vatican's nod to Netiquette may prove difficult. Writing confession – rather than listening to it – may be the harder temptation to resist in the tell-all, show-all digital age.

In a world gone digital, every day is now 1 January. 24/7 diary. The private curtain on confession has lifted and is now becoming its own electronic industry. In a megablink, we've gone from Dear Diary to Hello YouTube! The twenty-first-century diarist is part of Generation We – tech savvy and globally connected, keeping a diary on an iPhone or on internet sites like Open Diary. Janus, god of doorways, offers twenty-first-century portals: Facebook, MySpace, Twitter.

It's fitting that Italy, the country linked to some of the world's first diaries, should be innovating again. Janus-like, blogging priests can click to go backwards and forwards. To those preferring the pre-cyberspace world, say between 1335 and 1410, simply click on http://Datini.archiviodistato.prato.it to read the voluminous letters and accounting diary of Francesco Datini, merchant banker, cloth merchant and supplier of luxury goods. Stuck on how to begin a diary to compete with Datini? Cyberspace is the electronic diarist's endless emporium.

Consider just a few software options equipping diarists for the digital age. Among them: Diary Book, Diary Defender and Alive Diary. Far more specialised software packages include programs like Advance Diary. It offers features now standard in twentieth-century diary keeping, 'password protection; ability to insert photos; upload pages to your personal blog'. Personal Diary is software designed 'to store thoughts, feelings, memories, dreams, ideas'. Efficient Diary boasts 'a strong edit function', a boon to the self-censor. If the blank screen induces writer's block, then there's My Voice Diary, software created so diarists can dictate their entries. Still rattled? Then there's Anxiety Diary, 'a user-friendly electronic mental health system'.

It's not only the Vatican but neuroscientists who are giving diary keeping their benediction. A recent issue of *Scientific American* acknowledges, 'Besides serving as a stress-coping mechanism, expressive writing produces many physiological benefits. Research shows that it improves memory and sleep, boosts immune cell activity and reduces viral load in AIDS patients, and even speeds healing after surgery.' As millions of megabytes shoot into cyberspace, diarists are rearranging the very structure of neural cell activity.

The itch to record spans the scratch of a pen to the click of a keyboard. In just seventeen centuries, the world has gone from St Augustine writing his *Confessions* in AD 371 to Augustine's blog Blaugustine that ranks number 1,000 on the Writing–Express Yourself website. British artist and writer Natalie d'Arbeloff's cartoon alter ego Augustine 'illustrates the meaning of life, love, sex, self, God, people, philosophy, politics'. The blog's many links range from her webcomic to her own limited edition artist's books.

What has changed since Augustine in AD 371 isn't just the technology but the sheer volume of words. According to the Global Information Industry Center, in a twenty-four hour day, adults take in an average of 100,000 words of information – all of them outside of work. Adults spend 11.8 hours a day registering all those words. A whole new language is surfacing faster in diaries than in dictionaries: twitspeak, upload, friending. LOL or TMI diarists tweet across cyberspace.

No one (so far) has tabulated how many words are pinging daily in cyberspace. It's estimated that there are 200 million active blogs. Some 40–45 million iPhones, shaped like the earliest mass-produced Letts diaries, offer iDiary apps to edit and search for key words and find patterns in a diary. Just as twentieth-century visual images shifted from film to television screen, from computer to mobile phone screen, so diaries have grown from accounting books into journals and now into twenty-first-century blogs with cyber ads.

Inevitably, diaries continue to evolve along with the technology that serves – and shapes – mass culture. From a paper culture into a paperless world, the solitary diarist is now linked, free to read or post on thousands of diary sites – most with links to Facebook pages. Yet click on Open Diary or LiveJournal and you'll find virtual ads for the original software: 'custom journal books, writing pads. Leather notebooks and diaries.' Others offer 'high quality, extra smooth paper'. Whether keeping a hardbound or virtual journal, diarists can go to Dear Diary.net to store and keep it safe.

The Vatican decree is just one of the examples popping up daily of a world transformed by technology and driven by self-expression. A world where, for the diarist, those two are now forever linked virtually. From private to public, from individual to group-written entries, technology has not only affected but transformed self-expression. The diary has morphed into blogs, fragmented into Facebook, updated but then returned to its recording roots on Twitter with daily jottings, largely informational, of the events or thoughts.

In a culture of competing digital technology and limited attention spans, Twitter diaries were inevitable. It's estimated that 55 million tweets – the 140-character text messages – are sent monthly. ('Humbled' President Obama tweeted after learning he'd won the 2009 Nobel Prize.) Imagine how relieved past diarists would be to know that they weren't wasting a day (and still blank page) – they were simply tweeting.

'Wrote nothing.' Kafka. 1 June 1912.
'Slept sinfully.' Tolstoy. 9 December 1888.

If physician John Rutty had sent his 1753–4 'A Spiritual Diary and Soliloquies' as tweets, some might be mistaken as misspellings from all digital thumbs.

Rose too late: O the dull body!
Too idle in bed to-day: O flesh, thou clog
A little of the beast in drinking
A little swinish at dinner
A frappish cholerick day.

Twitter has done more than Freud to help diarists ditch the superego. Twitter's stray random thoughts are a low-stake digital entry. Tweets shatter the perfectionism that has prevented so many from keeping diaries. All those 'shoulds' have vanished: write only when having profound thoughts, no word misspelled. Robert Shields, the longest diarist in the Guinness Book of Records, died two years before Twitter. Sleeping in two-hour intervals between entries, he'd invented three dozen ways to describe needing to pee. His tweets could have provided others with updates of the best methods for every occasion. He could have used it to break his most sensational news: he had taped a nostril hair to a journal page so scientists could soon carry out genetic research on his diary mania.

In twenty-first-century cyberspace it's possible to create Diarist Avatar in Second Life, avoiding words altogether and still be a diarist. Since 1997, when internet servers first provided free homepages, cyberspace spawned a culture of diarists that now upload photos and customise their web pages. The endless ability to upload photos has led to an explosion of visual diaries, some created only from photographs, others modelled on Kurt Cobain's published diaries – words running along the edges of drawings. The advent of the visual diary also allows the diarist blogger to be social networker. On Flickr, the photo-sharing website, food diaries have increased tenfold since 2008. Over six million people now keep visual food diaries in the spirit of Brillat-Savarin's 'Tell me what you eat, and I will tell you what you are.'

Of all shifts in twenty-first-century cyberspace, the most striking phenomenon is the number of reluctant failed diarists who have turned ardent and skilful bloggers. Bloggers have assumed the mantle of traditional diary keeping – the daily entry – reinventing it in the process. The blogger's currency is self-expression; liberated by sharing, often trading on secrets, no longer constrained by them. The diary has come full circle. Yet the circle keeps expanding, twisting back on itself, less a circle than an ever-expanding helix. From traditional diary to cyberspace blog, from notebook to Facebook.

Consider Hal Niedzviecki's experiment in cyberspace.

I started blogging on January 16, 2008. I called my blog *The Peep Diaries: One Man's Journey Into Self-Exposure, Surveillance and the Future of Voyeurism*. I started blogging for two reasons. First, I wanted to see what it would be like to be a blogger, to write about my everyday life to an audience of total strangers… The second goal was to create a forum for ideas and developments in Peep culture.

While confessing he'd never kept a diary or a journal, the blog's title is a sly nod to the long history of diaries. As a blogger, he was no different from centuries of diarists who glimpsed a larger project emerging from the entries, in his case a book with the blog's soon familiar title.

As a blogger he'd become a digital diarist, feeling the same self-imposed pressure or duty to record his thoughts every day. His first post, written on a train to Kingston, Ontario, was a disaster. Too long. Worse, he realised, it had 'no single compelling idea or keyword for search engines to glom on to'. No audience.

No linking to the vast infrastructure of the blogosphere market. Frustrated by the blog's pathetic low post rate, he then experienced what centuries of diarists consciously avoided – criticism. One of the earliest posts chided him for not revealing more about himself – ironic given his blog's mission.

He faced the unique cyberspace challenge: shifting from digital diarist wary of prying eyes to a blogger's strategies to get *anyone*'s attention. He joined a galaxy of social networking sites and started posting to chat rooms. The blog linked to an electronic community giving him a sense of 'strangers rooting for me (as if I were a celebrity.)'. Ever since Jonathan Swift's 1710–13 *Journal to Stella*, his letter diary to friend Esther Johnson, diarists have thrived on having an ideal or intended reader. Niedzviecki was no different – finding comfort in the fact that others valued what he had to express.

Since the invention of paper, diarists have wanted to be seen. Admired. Forgiven. Transformed. In the twenty-first century that's now a collective activity. The truest wireless connection is the multi-friending diary – from Facebook or Twitter updates to group emails printed out into a journal. Nineteen centuries after Ts'ai Lun's invention, the digital diarist in a paperless world has endless resources. Visit Diarist Net for a directory of online diaries and journals. Visit DiaryLand to start a digital diary or link to others. Want to see what others have written since the first online diaries in 1995? Visit The Online Diary History Project.

Of course, there's an underside. As Hal Niedzviecki observes of one cyber sharer drawn to 'the possibilities of online community and the potential to develop audience and even celebrity, she also realizes that her online life is in many ways in contrast with her real life'. With 100 million signed up to Facebook worldwide, privacy and celebrity are now twin impulses. The digital diarist hopes to be simultaneously noticed and off limits. Gone are the days of da Vinci's reverse mirror writing or Pepys' cipher shorthand. We choose our firewalls, encrypting all technology gadgets but not the opinions we beam into cyber-space. What *isn't* posted on Facebook but kept in a private diary is now stored as confessional collateral.

The collision of public confession and private secrets had its first tipping point with pre-internet diarist Anaïs Nin. The notoriously private Nin wore a key to her current diary around her neck and stored her 1931 and 1974 journals in a New York bank vault. The diaries, published between 1966–74, won inter-national acclaim for their raw confessional power and their hint of erotica. To keep up with public appetite for confession and revelation, after her death her literary estate began a slow striptease of unpublished diary material: *Delta of Venus* and *Little Birds*, the erotica she co-wrote with novelist Henry Miller; *Incest: From a Journal of Love* and *Fire: From a Journal of Love*, the true story of her adult life with her long-absent father. Nin's belief that 'creation which cannot express itself becomes madness', inspired pre-internet diarists. Bloggers are now inspired by her diary entry: 'Shame is the lie someone told you about yourself.'

How Nin would have loved PostSecret, confession literally made into a contemporary art form. A writer anonymously dec-orates a postcard with a secret that's never been shared. It must be true and never spoken. Diarists can now raid their journals to confess or unburden themselves, the secret then scanned or sent to the online community project. If it requires instant revelation or response, diarists can go to Twitter to get updates via SMS.

While navigating in cyberspace, Hal Niedzvicki heard a con-stant blogger refrain: others think they know me, but they really don't. 'It's as if, having revealed everything, having laid bare every potential mystery, we want to pull back and reclaim that insoluble, essential something given away.' For centuries, diarists made peace with themselves in private. Now the cyber collective diary neatly shuts others out, publicly unfriending on Facebook. The digital diary has made an art of connection and disconnec-tion. Cyberbodies – the diary with benefits – is not for electronic diarist, Bitter Hag.

If you know me in real life, then chances are that you've stumbled on this site by accident. There's a reason I didn't give you this URL. I say this because this is where I do a lot of my venting about things I see and people I encounter in everyday life. If you are one of those people, you are likely to get your feelings hurt. It would be best for all concerned if you'd just turn around and leave now.

A whole new generation of digital diarists, though, have been raised on YouTube and reality shows. Boswell, patron diarist of celebrity and scandal, found clamouring for attention hard enough in 1774. Today millions of competing blogger diarists elbow for attention with public rants about private pain. Technological innovations increasingly allow the diarist to magnify themselves. A few diarists, simply born too early, were destined for YouTube. An ideal candidate is Hannah Cullwick, the Victorian domestic servant urged to keep diaries by her employer, poet Arthur Munby. He had a fetish for female servants, fascinated by details and photos of their domestic drudgery. They married in 1873, though he never publicly acknowledged their union.

Cyberspace's cardinal rule now is: show don't hide. With its constant Twitter updates, the digital diary imitates 24/7 news cycles, blurring the line between private and public. Gossip – that mainstay of centuries of diaries – is sent rather than stored. Unreliable facts spread faster than computer viruses. That's true even in pre-cyberspace journals such as explorer Richard E. Byrd's 1925–7 diary and notebooks. On 9 May 1926 Richard E. Byrd had the honour of being the first to fly over the North Pole. His diary recorded the preparations and navigational calculations. After his death in 1957, his co-pilot confessed weather had made the North Pole route impossible. So they circled the horizon, unseen by reporters, and landed only when enough time had passed.

In today's Alice in Wonderland world of shrinking print and expanding megabytes, the diarist blogger has a double advantage.

Social networking opens up diary support – and topics. Visit DiaryLand and up pop virtual ads for 'Diary of a Bipolar'. The online diary community Open Diary offers 'diary circles' focused on a single issue – abuse, adoption, addiction. Collectively, the digital diarist strives for what Scott in Antarctica or Livingstone in malarial Africa showed – resilience. The instinct to record is primal, as neuroscientists are now discovering, hardwired to the brain.

Journal keeping, long condemned or marginalised as 'therapy', in fact has a scientific basis. Dr Neil Neimark makes the psychoneuroimmunological case for diary as support group, erasing shame or trauma.

> Every thought we have, every feeling we experience, every attitude we hold translates itself into a complex pattern of chemical release and nerve cell firing. These complex patterns result in the release of neuropeptides, which are chemical messengers of thought, feeling, attitude and belief. When we journal about traumatic life events and reconstruct the painful thoughts and images associated with those events, we are, in fact, changing the very essence of our biochemistry. We are, in fact, changing the very structure and pattern of brain cell activity.

To achieve this, twenty-first-century diarists are rediscovering the eighteenth-century tradition of keeping gratitude journals. What started with Quaker diaries has become a mainstay of longtime journal keepers like Oprah. It focuses what psychologists call 'intentional activity', the brain instilling positive habits. Scientists have long proven its health benefits, from coping with arthritis to post-breast cancer recovery. The mind / body connection was long borne out in John Wesley's eight-volume 1720–91 gratitude-based diaries. At eighty-five, he hadn't lost a night's sleep in his life or suffered depression for more than fifteen minutes since childhood. W.N.P. Barbellion, a naturalist living in London, was plagued by debilitating paralysis, meticulously recorded in his 1889–1919 *The Journal of Disappointed Man*. As a blogger, he'd have a sure-fire hit.

'I always think of Samuel Pepys as a sort of proto-blogger,' notes Julie Powell, author of *Julie & Julia: My Year of Cooking Dangerously*, the book that emerged from a blog she kept to cure misery. Pepys' diaries are among a dozen books she cites as instrumental in helping her make that leap. Just as Boswell launched himself via Samuel Johnson, so Powell did with Julia Child. On her 'crap laptop', she started her Julie/Julia blog, devoting a year to cooking her way through 524 recipes in the 1961 classic, *Mastering the Art of French Cooking*. She found herself in a parallel universe, government secretary by day, foodie blogger by night. Wormholes, she concedes, warp memory, 'but there was no question I was in a different place. The old universe had been subjugated under the tyranny of entropy. There, I was just a secretary-shaped confederation of atoms, fighting the inevitability of mediocrity and decay. But here, in Juliaverse, the laws of thermodynamics had been turned on their heads. Here, energy was never lost, merely converted.'

Pepys' entry, 'Dined alone; sad for want of company and know not how to eat alone', could easily have inspired her blog odyssey. Any cyber diarist can visit Pepysdiary.com hoping inspiration will follow. Or jumpstart creativity each morning with 'This date, from Henry David Thoreau's Journal', blogthoreau@blogspot.com. Or download Project Gutenberg's *The Notebooks of Leonardo Da Vinci*. Or read Scott's Antarctic journals using the British Library's digital 'Turning the Pages' system. Food historian Mary Gunderson read Lewis and Clark's epic journals to see what they ate. Their thirteen volumes yielded her book, *The Food Journal of Lewis & Clark: Recipes for an Expedition*.

The twenty-first-century diarist faces brave new frontiers stranger than any Lewis and Clark knew. Does the digital diarist own rights to his self-expression *and* his anonymity? Privacy law is panicked by today's tell-all, know-all cyberspace. The

Electronic Frontier Foundation at the University of California at Berkeley sued the CIA for using social networking sites to search for information. Can a cover agent have a public diary with his or her real name? A moot point for the virtual shared diary, couples using Facebook like the Tolstoys once used their diaries – airing spats in the court of public opinion.

Blogging envy now mirrors private regrets expressed by earlier diarists. In 1939 Virginia Woolf lamented being unable to 'compete with the compression & lucidity & logic of Gide writing his journal'. Today bloggers invoke Oscar Wilde on secrets for their mission statement, 'If I didn't write them down I should probably forget all about them.' Or cite Fanny Burney, 'to whom dare I reveal my private opinion of my nearest relations? My secret thoughts of my dearest friends? My own hopes, fear, reflections and dislikes?'

Twenty-first-century diary keeping is now that perfect mix of confession, self-expression and moral improvement by sharing rather than concealing. In its ever-evolving history, diaries surface in the age ready for their revelations. Pepys' diaries weren't deciphered until 1825; Boswell's published only in 1950. On the cusp of New Year's 2010, as diarists bought new journals, a long-secret journal was published. Its pages had virtually invented the collective unconscious of cyberspace and the 'individuation' diarists seek. *The Red Book, Liber Novus*, Carl Jung's zealously guarded private journal, surfaced fifty years after his death. Biographers and bloggers had long hoped to read the journal he wrote, revised and illustrated between 1914 and 1930. It offered clues to the wellspring of his work – insights he and his former mentor Freud had gained about creativity, neuroses and self-transformation.

The Red Book embodies and combines every form a diary has taken over the centuries – from reflective record of conscience to inward travel journal to visual diary – its pages illustrated with dragons challenging inner demons or with a tree symbolising the Book of Life. In a full-page rave review, memoirist Kathryn

Harrison noted that this latest of published journals 'not only reminds us of the importance of introspection, but also offers a guide to separating the self from the spirit of a time that would have astonished and offended Jung with its endless trivial distractions, its blogs and tweets and endless chiming cellphones...' Like all private diaries, it offers 'an inquiry into what it means to be human'.

Foursquare, a mobile social network, now allows users to tell others where they are located at that precise moment. Standing on a busy street corner, digitally equipped, diarists are still writing, still locating coordinates, still trying to connect.

Bibliography

Innovators

Boswell, James. *The Journals of James Boswell*, selected by John Wain. New Haven: Yale University Press. 1991.

Dee, John. *The Diaries of John Dee*, ed. Edward Fenton. Oxfordshire: Day Books. 1998.

Evelyn, John. *The Diary of John Evelyn*, ed. E.S. de Beer. New York: Oxford University Press. 1959.

Landucci, Luca. *A Florentine Diary 1450–1516*. New York: Dutton. 1927.

Niccolini, Ginevra di Camugliano. *Chronicles of a Florentine Family 1200–1470*. London: Jonathan Cape. 1933.

Pepys, Samuel. *The Diaries of Samuel Pepys*, ed. Richard Le Gallienne. New York: Modern Library. 2003.

Travel and Explorer Diaries

Dallam, Thomas. *Early Voyages and Travels in the Levant: The Diaries of Master Thomas Dallam 1599–1600*, ed. J. Theodore Bent. London: Printed for the Hakluyt Society. 1893.

Darwin, Charles. *The Voyage of the Beagle*. New York: P.F. Collier. 1909.

Fabri, Felix. *Wanderings of Felix Fabri*, trans. Aubrey Stewart. 2 vols. London: The Library of the Palestine Pilgrims' Text Society. 1896.

Battuta, Ibn. *Travels in Asia and Africa, 1325–1354*, trans. H.A.R. Gibb. London: G. Routledge & Sons. 1929.

Lewis, Meriwether and Clark, John. *The Journals of Lewis and Clark*, selected by John Bakeless. New York: Penguin. 2002.

Lewis, Meriwether and Clark, John. *The Journals of the Lewis and Clark Expedition*, ed. Gary E. Moulton. 13 vols. Omaha: University of Nebraska Press. 2002.

Scott, Robert Falcon. *Journals: Captain Scott's Last Expedition*, ed. Max Jones. New York: Oxford University Press. 2006.

Thoreau, Henry David. *Journals*, ed. Bradford Torrey. Boston: Houghton Mifflin. 1906.

Thoreau, Henry David. *Walden*. Boston: Houghton Mifflin. 2004.

Torkington, Richard. *Ye Oldest Diarie of Englysshe Travell*, ed. W.J. Loftie. London: Field & Tuer. 1884.

Writers, Artists and Creative Diaries

Burney, Fanny. *Journals and Letters*, selected by Peter Sabor. New York: Penguin. 2001.

Camus, Albert. *Notebooks 1935–1942*, trans. Philip Thody. New York: Modern Library. 1965.

Da Vinci, Leonardo. *The Notebooks of Leonardo da Vinci*, ed. Irma A. Richter.
    New York: Oxford University Press. 1998.

Degas, Edgar. *The Notebooks of Edgar Degas*, 2 vols, ed. Theodore Reff.
    Oxford: Clarendon Press. 1976.

Delacroix, Eugene. *The Journals of Eugene Delacroix*, trans. Walter Pach.
    New York: Crown. 1948.

Gauguin, Paul. *Intimate Journals*, trans. Van Wyck Brooks.
    New York: Dover. 1997.

Kafka, Franz. *The Diaries of Franz Kafka*, ed. Max Brod.
    New York: Shocken. 1948.

Mansfield, Katherine. *The Journal of Katherine Mansfield, Definitive Edition*,
    ed. J.M. Murry. London: Constable. 1954.

Plath, Sylvia. *The Journals of Sylvia Plath 1950–62*, ed. Karen V. Kukil.
    London: Faber and Faber. 2000.

Sarton, May. *Journal of a Solitude*. New York: Norton. 1973.

Sarton, May. *At Seventy: A Journal*. New York: Norton. 1984.

Sarton, May. *After the Stroke: A Journal*. New York: Norton. 1988.

Tolstoy, Leo. *Tolstoy's Diaries*, ed. R.F. Christian. London:
    The Athlone Press. 1985.

Tolstoy, Sofia. *The Diaries of Sophia Tolstoy*, ed. O.A. Golinenko,
    trans. Cathy Porter. New York: Random House. 1985.

Woolf, Virgina. *A Writer's Diary*, ed. Leonard Woolf.
    London: Hogarth Press. 1953.

Woolf, Virginia. *The Diary of Virginia Woolf*, 5 vol, ed. Anne Oliver Bell.
    New York: Harcourt Brace. 1976.

War Diaries

Chestnut, Mary. *Mary Chestnut's Civil War*, ed. C. Vann Woodward.
    New York: Yale University Press. 1981.

Frank, Anne. *The Diary of a Young Girl*. New York: Doubleday. 1991.

Hillesum, Etty. *An Interrupted Life: the Diaries of Etty Hillesum 1941–1943*.
    New York: Washington Square Press. 1985.

Klemperer, Victor. *To the Bitter End: the Diaries of Victor Klemperer, 1942–1945*.
    London: Weidenfeld & Nicolson. 1999.

Origo, Iris. *War in Val D'Orcia, 1943–1944: A Diary*. Boston: D.R. Godine. 1984.

Sassoon, Siegfried. *Siegfried Sassoon Diaries 1915–1918*, ed. Rupert Hart-Davis.
    London: Faber and Faber. 1985.

Cyberspace and Digital Diarist

Jung, Carl, *The Red Book: Liber Novus*. New York: Norton. 2009.

Niedzviecki, Hal. *The Peep Diaries*. San Francisco: City Lights Books. 2009.

Of General Interest

Kelly, Kevin (foreword). *The 1000 Journals Project*. San Francisco: Chronicle Books. 2007.

Mallon, Thomas. *A Book of One's Own*. New York: Ticknor & Fields. 1984.

Matthews, William. *British Diaries: an annotated bibliography of British Diaries written between 1441 and 1942*. Los Angeles: University of California Press. 1950.

Spalding, P.A. *Self-Harvest*. London: Independent Press. 1949.

Biographical note

Alexandra Johnson is the author of *The Hidden Writer*, winner of the PEN/Jerard Award for Nonfiction. She is also the author of *Leaving a Trace*. Oprah chose a chapter from it for *O Magazine*. Her essays have been published in numerous anthologies. Her work has also appeared in *The New York Times Book Review*, *The Nation*, *Ms Magazine*, among numerous national publications. A recognised diary expert, Johnson has been featured extensively on National Public Radio and television. She is often interviewed in the increasingly linked cyberspace and diary networks. She has taught at Harvard, Wellesley College and in the MFA Program in Creative Writing at Lesley University.

Acknowledgements

A good portion of this book was written in The Spalding-Naumburg Room in Harvard's Loeb Library. It provided an ideal space to think about a millennium of diaries. Harvard's Widener Library, that eight-mile underground literary city, has on its shelves every one of the diaries mentioned in this book. From Dee to Dallam, Landucci to Livingstone, Thoreau to Sassoon, these and countless other diaries are part of the library's vast collection. I am grateful once again to Widener and its staff.

I would like to thank Ellie Robins for the invitation to write *A Brief History of Diaries*. My deepest thanks go to Martha Pooley, a superb editor, whose meticulous care in reading and responding to the ms. at successive stages is greatly appreciated. May all authors have an editor as gracious, thorough and intelligent as Martha.

HESPERUS PRESS

Hesperus Press is committed to bringing near what is far – far both in space and time. Works written by the greatest authors, and unjustly neglected or simply little known in the English-speaking world, are made accessible through new translations and a completely fresh editorial approach. Through these classic works, the reader is introduced to the greatest writers from all times and all cultures.

For more information on Hesperus Press, please visit our website: **www.hesperuspress.com**